Van Gogh

ELEANOR MARRACK

CHARTWELL BOOKS, INC.

Published by
CHARTWELL BOOKS, INC.
A Division of BOOK SALES, INC.
110 Enterprise Avenue
Secaucus, New Jersey 07094

Produced by
Brompton Books Corp.
15 Sherwood Place
Greenwich, CT 06830

ISBN 1-55521-763-X

Printed in Hong Kong

LIST OF PLATES

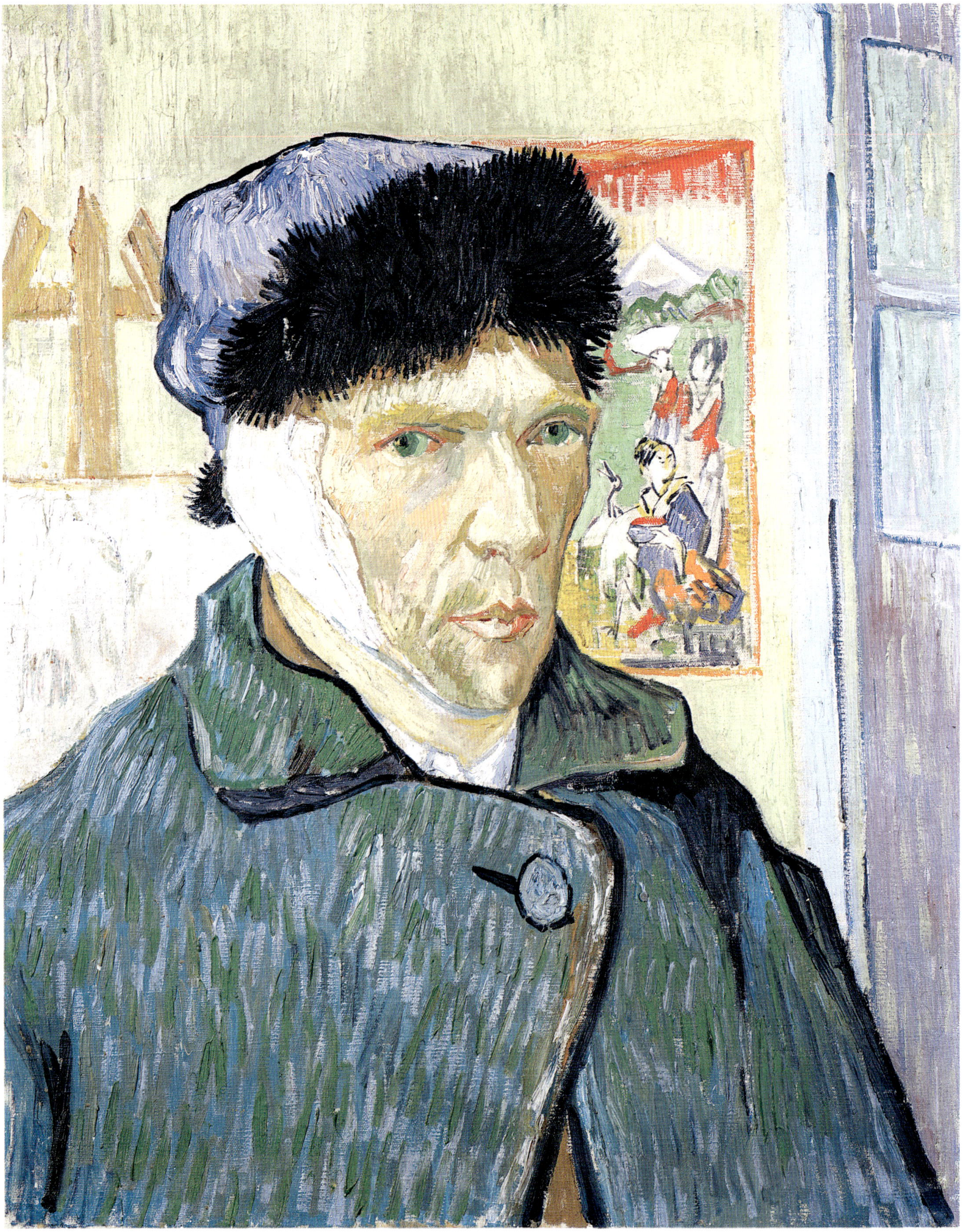

Self Portrait with Bandaged Ear, January 1889
Oil on canvas, 23½×19¼ inches (60×49cm)
Courtauld Institute Galleries, London

VINCENT VAN GOGH

1853-1890

Art historians, psychologists and investors have all had a field day with van Gogh. In the heady confident 1980s, his work became an index of art market buoyancy as each succeeding sale produced a new record price, culminating in the staggering $49 million realized by *Irises* (1889) in November 1987. Intense historical research into every stage of his artistic and psychological development has produced a welter of not always consistent evidence. The notion of van Gogh as the struggling, isolated artist whose work is the unmediated expression of an inspired but tormented spirit in direct response to nature is gradually losing currency, as the extent to which his art was a conscious creation becomes clear. And yet the art historical construct of the artist as anguished genius, of creativity as an abnormal psychological phenomenon, continues to thrive. The fact of van Gogh's creativity cannot be doubted, and yet its expression was restricted to the last quarter of his life and all the best known work, including every image reproduced here, dates from between 1885, five years after his decision to become an artist at the age of 27, and his death in 1890. During almost the whole of this period van Gogh was living in France – he moved to Paris in February 1886 – but his Dutch roots played an equally formative role in his development as artist.

Vincent William van Gogh was born on March 30, 1853, the eldest of three brothers and three sisters. His father was a not particularly successful parson and the north Brabant village of Groot Zundert in southern Holland, where van Gogh spent his early years, was a rural backwater. The family as a whole was predominantly Hague-based, however, and included three art dealers. At the age of 16 van Gogh started work at the Hague gallery of the international art dealers Goupil et cie, and it seems that this was the result of family connection – his uncle Vincent was a partner in the firm – rather than any particular preference on his part. Goupil's particular strength lay in the sale of prints and reproductions, mainly of French academic, genre and landscape, although an increasingly large number of original works by contemporary Dutch artists were also being sold. Thus the young van Gogh was introduced to a wide range of artistic reference and he became an avid collector of prints, illustrations from magazines, photographic reproductions and, at a later date, fine art prints, especially the then fashionable Japanese woodblock prints. He also began to develop his own tastes, including an enthusiasm for the new wave of Dutch artists known as The Hague School. Hague School painters combined opposition to classical conventions and an interest in landscape painting for its own sake with a romantically nostalgic view of pre-industrial Holland. Van Gogh's early interest in sentiment-imbued landscape and the artist's direct response to nature was to emerge as a major feature of his own mature work.

After four years Vincent was sent to work in the London office of Goupil but, interestingly, this did not significantly enlarge his artistic tastes. He preferred the landscapes of Constable and the narrative work of Millais to the late Pre-Raphaelites or Rossetti, although he did develop an interest in English graphic art, with its concern with social issues. The London months were also notable for the first signs of mental instability, precipitated by Vincent's unrequited love for his landlady's daughter. Increasingly he took refuge in an intense religious fervor, a vocational commitment both to help the unfortunate and to redeem himself through self-mortification. By January 1876, after two periods in the Paris offices of Goupil, where he explored the works of Millet and Corot but still seemed to avoid the avant-garde, van Gogh's alienation from commerce became so marked that he was given notice.

The following few years saw an unsettled van Gogh throw himself with temporary enthusiasm into a series of professions. First he returned to England as an unpaid school assistant, then he began to train for the ministry but found academic study uncongenial. Finally, in 1878, he became a lay preacher among the impoverished miners in the grim Borinage district of Belgium, sharing all his food and clothing with the unfortunate in a literal interpretation of Christ's teaching that again led to his dismissal. He stayed in the Borinage until 1880, supported by his younger brother Theo, who had followed Vincent into the world of art dealing with more success and remained both a financial and a spiritual support to him for the remainder of his life; much of our knowledge of Vincent's psychological development comes from the regular letters exchanged by the brothers.

During his last year in the Borinage, van Gogh made a growing number of sketches of the miners with whom he lived, and his decision to become an artist is usually dated to a letter in August 1880 in which he announced this intention to Theo. He left the Borinage and went to Brussels, throwing himself into his studies with characteristic intensity and determination and rekindling his enthusiasm for graphic artists such as Luke Fildes and Frank Holl, whose work appeared in *The Graphic* and *The Illustrated London News*. He saw their powerful images of urban poverty as paralleling the country peasant themes of Millet which he had seen in Paris.

In April 1881, after six months' study of perspective and anatomy in Brussels, Vincent returned home to his father's parsonage at Etten. His earliest works, dating from this time, explore his continuing sense of the poetic beauty of rural labor in expressive landscapes, inspired above all by the work of Millet. After eight months, however, his insensitive and unsuccessful attempts to form a relationship with his widowed cousin Kee Vos tried the family patience to the point where he had to leave. He moved to The Hague, where he worked under the guidance of Anton Mauve, a member of The Hague School of artists and Vincent's cousin by marriage. Vincent's first fully resolved oil painting, *Girl Under Trees* (1882), is self-consciously modeled on Mauve's woodland motifs and techniques. At the same time he set up home with a prostitute, Sien Hoornik, who became his model and the subject of some of his best known early drawings, such as the lithograph *Sorrow* (1882). After a year the relationship deteriorated and Vincent fell ill, was rescued by his family and again moved home financed by Theo, this time to Neunen. The majority of paintings from this time are of the surrounding landscape and portraits of peasants, culminating in *The Potato Eaters* (1885), which combines a rural theme with the harsh realism of graphic art and an element of Christian symbolism in its near-sacramental image of a peasant supper.

By autumn 1885 van Gogh felt the need to compensate for his lack of formal training as an artist, and moved to Antwerp on the advice of Mauve to study at the Academy. Academic instruction proved to have little to offer such an individualistic temperament, but the great altarpieces by Peter Paul Rubens in the cathedral inspired the first major modification in van Gogh's hitherto dark-toned palette. He had already started to use more blue, but now he also experimented with red and his palette lightened. Antwerp did not long satisfy his desire for new artistic experiences. Theo was in Paris, and becoming increasingly involved in promoting and selling impressionist paintings; the correspondence between the two brothers had broadened in the course of 1885 to include the relative merits of realism, naturalism and romanticism, and Vincent wanted to study all these movements at first hand. He badgered Theo to let him come to Paris, and finally forced his brother's hand by arriving at the Gare du Nord in early March 1886.

Theo already at this time handled the work of Monet, Pissarro and Sisley whenever he could obtain them, and was soon to take up that of Gauguin and Toulouse Lautrec. Vincent, however, had hitherto been sheltered from the avant-garde and had written of Impressionism as something he had not seen or properly understood. His interest in the French historical painter Delacroix's use of color led him to explore various theories of complementary color and contrasts, which also formed the basis for Seurat's pointillist work. At first, however, van Gogh was disappointed with what he found in Paris, writing to his sister that on first view the Impressionists seemed 'ugly, sloppily and badly painted, badly drawn, of a poor color; everything that is miserable.' His early Paris works, mainly self-portraits and still lifes, are in the same somber colors and broad faceted strokes as his Brussels and Antwerp pictures.

The following winter saw a major development in his work and a rapid absorption of wide-ranging influences. Among the older Impressionists his only significant contact was Pissarro, to whom Theo introduced him and who explained to him the theory and techniques of his own paintings. Van Gogh's first truly impressionist paintings, such as *Riverbank in Springtime*, were made early in 1887. Theo also took him to see the color merchant *père* Tanguy, who supplied many of the Impressionists, often accepting paintings as payment, and who became a firm admirer of van Gogh's work. Equally influential were his friendships with younger and more radical painters such as Paul Signac, an advocate of pointillism, and Emile Bernard, who used flat, unmodulated areas of bright color and strong outlines in a style which he described as 'Cloissonism'. The three spent much of the spring and summer of 1887 painting at Asnières, a northern suburb of Paris (*Bridge at Asnières*) and works such as *Interior of a Restaurant* show van Gogh tentatively adopting the pointillist dot-stroke developed by Seurat.

The final element in the crucial artistic synthesis of early 1887 was the inspiration van Gogh drew from Japanese woodblock prints, by then an established and powerful influence on European art. These highly colored images of landscapes, actors, courtesans and mythological subjects, with their unconventional viewpoints, flat areas of color and black outlines, played a major part in van Gogh's intensified use of color. His own free transcription of a a woodblock print, *Japonaiserie – Bridge in the Rain (after Hiroshige)*, includes stridently contrasting green and red borders containing vertical panels of Japanese text. Equally important for his later landscape work was the influence of Japanese prints on his drawing style and brushwork.

Van Gogh first met Gauguin in fall 1886, and his decision to move to Provence in February 1888 was partly inspired by Gauguin's highly colored descriptions of the primitive society of Martinique, where he spent much of 1887. The sheer pace of Parisian life, the multiple artistic strands to which van Gogh was exposed there and his own productivity – he painted over 230 pictures in two years – had also taken a toll. In the hot, primitive south he hoped to find the color schemes of Delacroix, the incisive outlines of Japanese prints, the landscapes he had seen in the canvases by Cézanne at Tanguy's, and the slower, more harmonious qualities of rural life to which he continued to be attracted. Arriving in Arles, he set instantly and feverishly to work and soon wrote to Theo: 'What I learned in Paris is leaving me and I am returning to the ideas I had . . . before I knew the impressionists . . . instead of trying to reproduce exactly what I have before my eyes, I use color more arbitrarily so as to express myself forcibly.' He was shocked by the strength of color and clarity of atmosphere he found, and recorded them in a series of powerful landscapes, such as *Landscape with the Plains of Crau* and *Haystacks in Provence*. He ranged widely to find new subjects, visiting the Rhône delta to paint fishing craft in *Boats on the Beach at Saintes-Maries*, and finding Dutch-style wooden bridges straddling the Rhône on the southern edge of Arles for *The Bridge of Langlois*. So intense was the inspiration that van Gogh drew from his new surroundings that he finished over 200 canvases in the first fifteen months of his stay in the south, but sold none of them and lived in considerable poverty, dependent as ever on the patient Theo.

Until October 1888 Vincent lived alone in Arles, drawing his main intellectual stimulation from the correspondence with Theo and with Bernard, who kept him in touch with the avant-garde. His painting continued to concentrate on his own immediate response to the south; by the end of the summer he had completed his series of Wheatfields and Sunflowers (*Fourteen Sunflowers*) and was beginning to focus on the townscape of Arles itself (*The Café Terrace, Arles at Night*). In the course of the summer he moved from his lodging in a cafe to a four-roomed house on the Place Lamartine (*Yellow House in Arles*) and became anxious for like-minded company, reviving a long-cherished dream of establishing an artistic colony. Theo was persuaded to finance a plan for Gauguin to join van Gogh in Arles, and in expectation of Gauguin's arrival van Gogh painted one of his most tranquil and contented pictures, *Van Gogh's Bedroom.*

Initially Gauguin's presence proved a stimulus and led van Gogh to modify the working practices he had established in the course of the summer. Many of Gauguin's paintings in Arles were effectively a critique of van Gogh's methods, particularly his stress on a direct confrontation with nature. For Gauguin, memory and imagination were essential to artistic expression; he perceived experience recollected and interpreted as more intellectually substantial than fidelity to the natural and was never able to identify wholeheartedly with impressionism. He emphasized the decorative, anti-naturalistic qualities of painting as a means of expressing the artist's subjectivity. Under his influence, van Gogh was persuaded to paint from dream and memory, and to renew his exploration of the exaggerated colors and idiosyncratic spatial values of Japanese prints. In *The Sower* of late November 1888, the flat quality of the background, the silhouette-like figure and the angled tree are all inspired by Japanese prints, while the subject, a metaphorical representation of the seasonal cycle of rural life which recalls some of Vincent's earliest work, is based on imagination rather than observation.

Temperamentally the two artists were less than well matched, however, and in the course of December, when bad weather kept them indoors, they drank heavily and argued bitterly about their fundamentally incompatible artistic viewpoints. Tension came to a head on December 23; it seems that yet another quarrel precipitated van Gogh into some form of breakdown. Gauguin, fearing for his safety, moved to a hotel and van Gogh, left alone in a state of turmoil, cut off his earlobe and took it to the local brothel, perhaps expecting Gauguin to be there. The following day Gauguin returned to Paris and van Gogh spent three days in the local hospital in delirium. He continued to paint feverishly after his discharge, including a number of portraits of neighbors, but was again hospitalized in mid-February after another serious collapse, possibly linked to Theo's announcement of his impending marriage.

In May 1889 van Gogh voluntarily entered an asylum near St Rémy, about twelve miles east of Arles, under the care of Dr Peyron, who told him that he was suffering from epilepsy. The true nature of his illness continues to cause debate and may well have been at least in part hereditary – one of his sisters spent the last 40 years of her life in an asylum and there is some evidence that Theo, in a state of mental collapse, killed himself. The view that the frenzied nature of his painting is an expression of his mental disorder is now discredited, however. His exaggerations of line, color and texture can be seen to have been developed for artistic purposes recognizable to his contemporaries.

At first he was confined within the hospital walls and in May and June produced a group of pictures exploring the motifs available. *Mountainous Landscape, View from St Paul's Hospital* was painted from the windows of his room, while the *Irises* he found growing in the overgrown garden, and painted them in close-up with virtually no background. In June he was allowed outside the grounds and explored the surrounding countryside, more arid and infertile than the rich plains of Arles. The resulting group of pictures, including *Starry Night* as well as landscapes with cypresses and olive trees, are sometimes seen as expressing a sense of the benevolent order of nature, rather than the anguish more normally associated with his work. A further breakdown in late summer prevented him from painting for several months but the *Self-Portrait* painted soon after his recovery shows him both returning to and moving on from the concerns of the midsummer, with its oscillating line and contrast of blue with its complementary orange. When winter came and he could no longer paint outside, van Gogh resorted to the collection of reproductions he had begun at the very outset of his career as an art dealer. *Noon or the Siesta (after Millet)* draws on Millet's peasant pictures and *Pietà (after Delacroix)* on New Testament subjects by Delacroix.

After a year at St Rémy van Gogh was anxious to move north again, to be near his brother and to paint with a different palette. At Pissarro's suggestion Theo arranged for him to lodge in Auvers, northwest of Paris, under the supervision of Dr Paul Gachet, a homeopathic doctor and friend of several of the Impressionists. Again Vincent embarked on a burst of strenuous activity, producing some 70 canvases during the last 70 days of his life. Despite his earlier intention of returning to a cooler northern palette, there is no lessening in the intensity of color in these late works but the quality is variable and the brushwork is sometimes brittle and arbitrary. Some images seem to quiver and take on a life of their own, as in the portrait of *Dr Paul Gachet* or *The Church at Auvers*. The vast space of the Auvers wheatfields inspired long thin canvases totally devoid of human reference, in which only the lowering clouds and the menacing crows move across the landscape. These empty vistas are often associated with the artist's final suicidal despair. On July 27, just two months after his arrival in Auvers, van Gogh shot himself in a field, then walked back to his lodging. He remained conscious throughout the next day and finally died on the morning of July 29 with Theo at his side. Just before, Theo had written to his wife: '. . . poor fellow, very little happiness fell to his share, and no illusions are left. The burden grows too heavy at times, he feels so alone.'

Van Gogh sold only one painting during his lifetime and his work was hardly known to the art world at the time of his death. In the first decade of the twentieth century, however, he was hailed by the new generation of Expressionist artists as a founding force, with his emotional, expressive use of line and color, while for Picasso he was the originator of the modern tradition of artistic individualism. Today he is recognized, alongside Cézanne and Gauguin, as the greatest of Post-Impressionist artists.

Wheatfields at Auvers, July 1890
Oil on canvas, 29×36¼ inches (73.5×92cm)
Neue Pinakothek, Munich

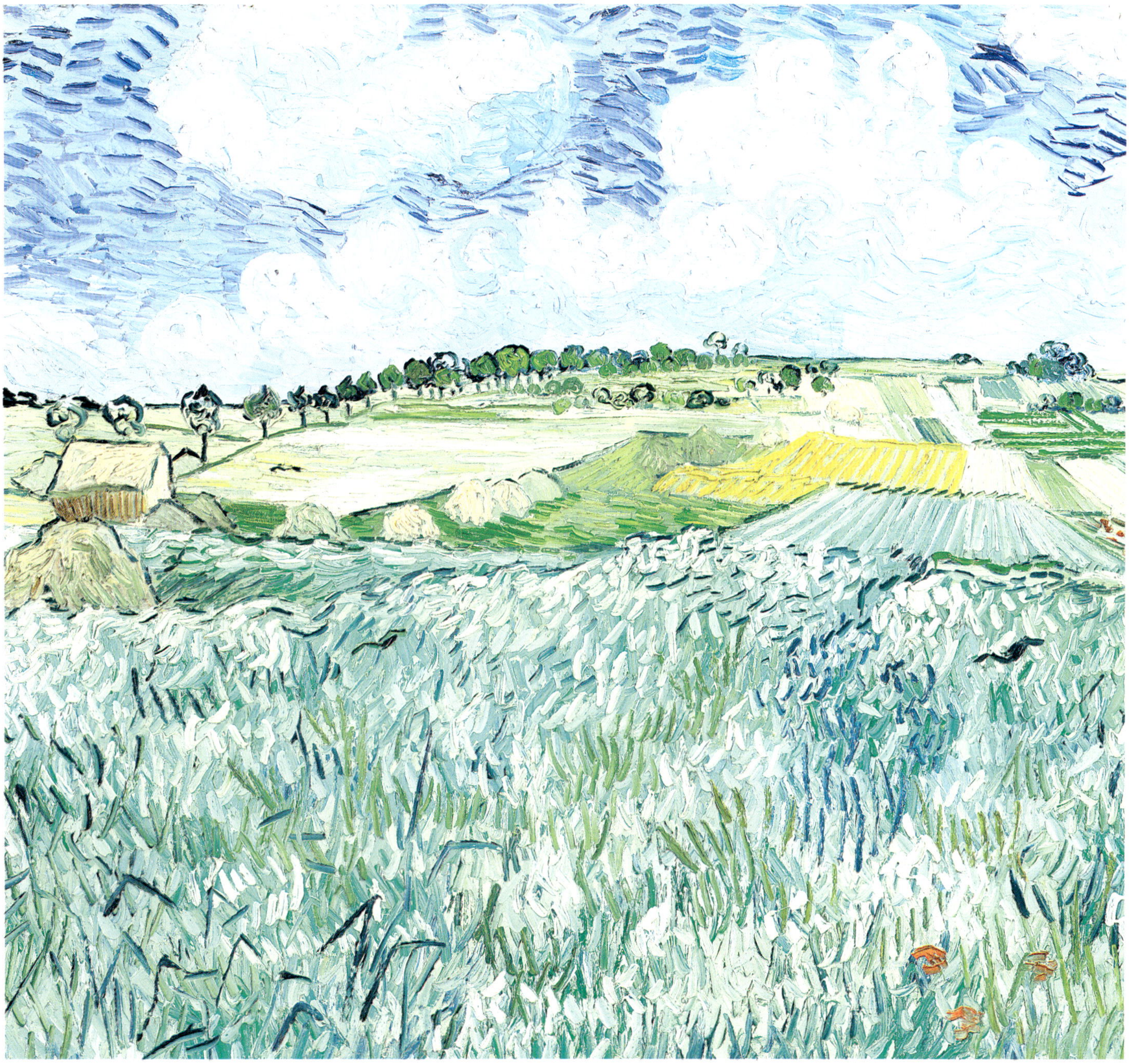

THE POTATO EATERS, April-May 1885
Oil on canvas, 32¼×45 inches (82×114cm)
Rijksmuseum Vincent van Gogh, Amsterdam

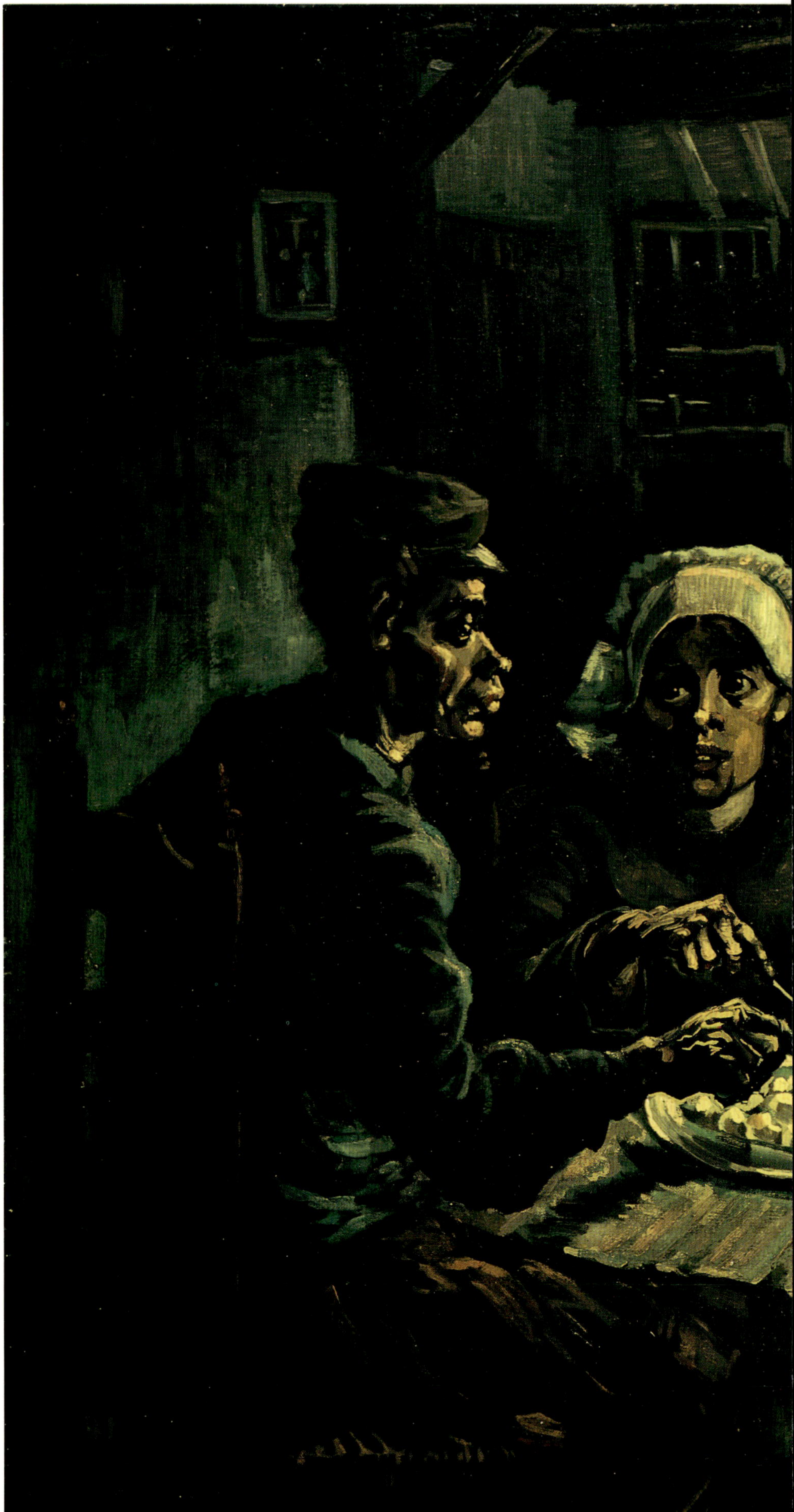

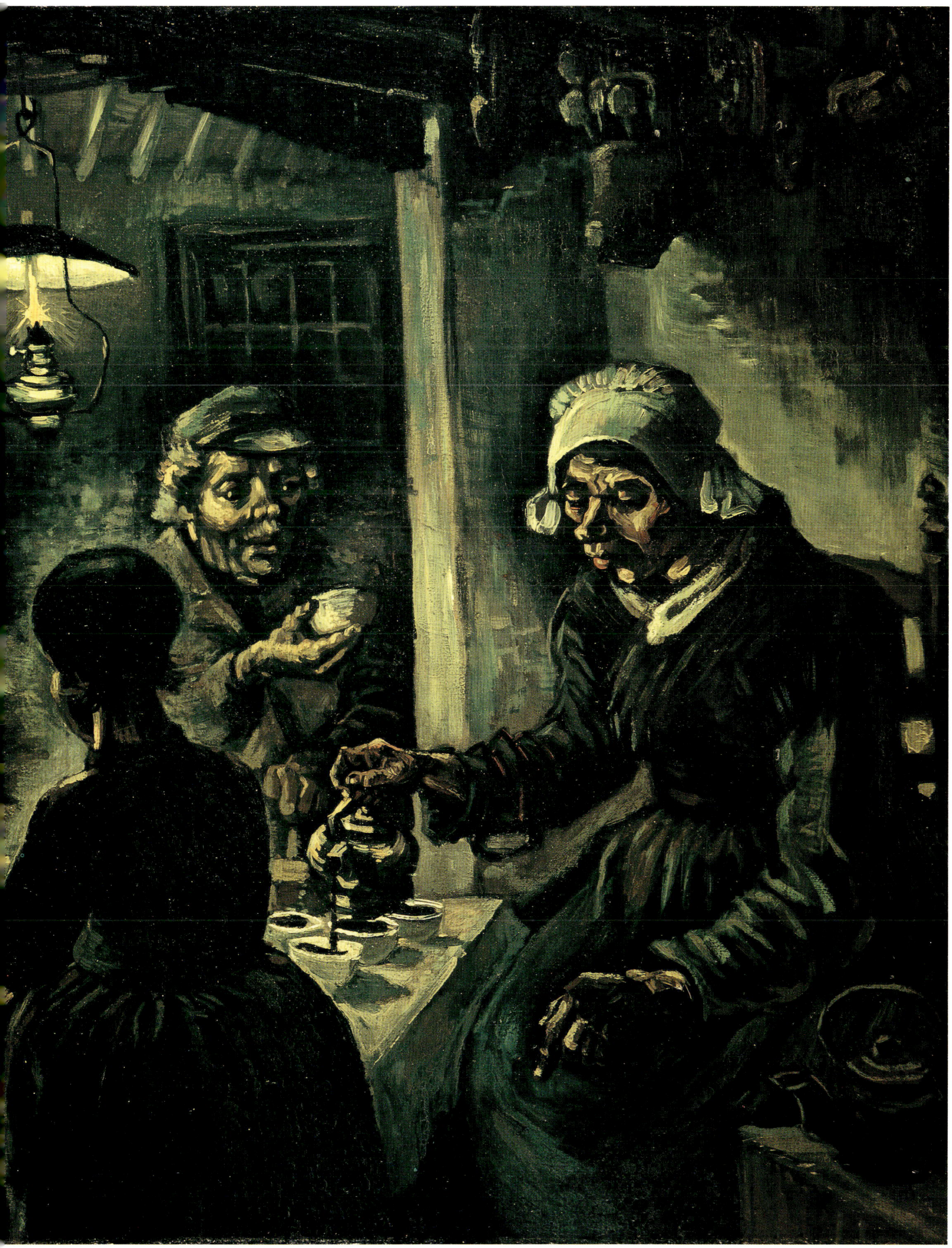

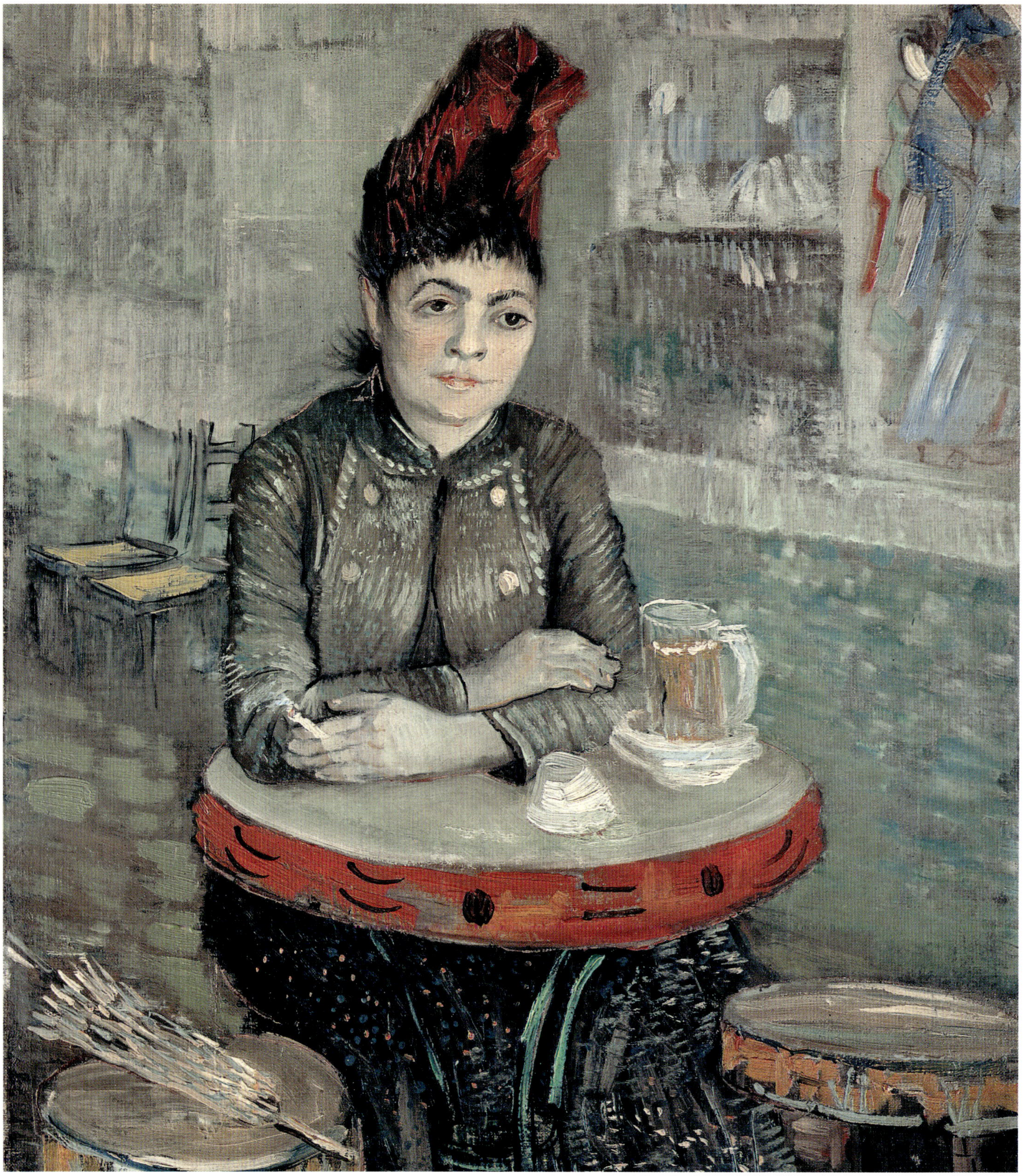

Woman at the Café du Tambourin, February 1887
Oil on canvas, 21¾×18¼ inches (55.5×46.5cm)
Rijksmuseum Vincent van Gogh
Amsterdam

RIVERBANK IN SPRINGTIME, Summer 1887
Oil on canvas, 19×22½ inches (50×60cm)
Dallas Museum of Arts

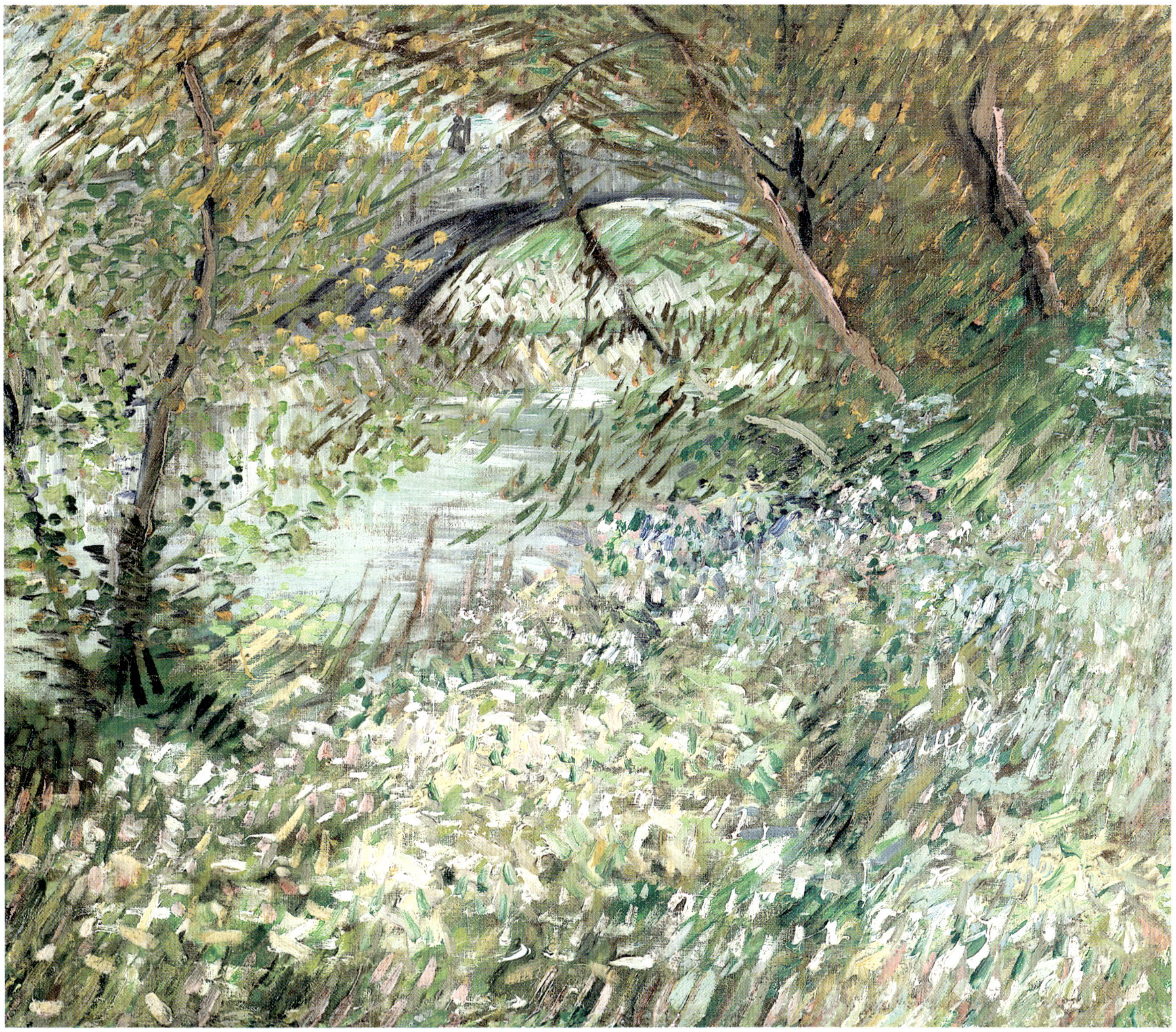

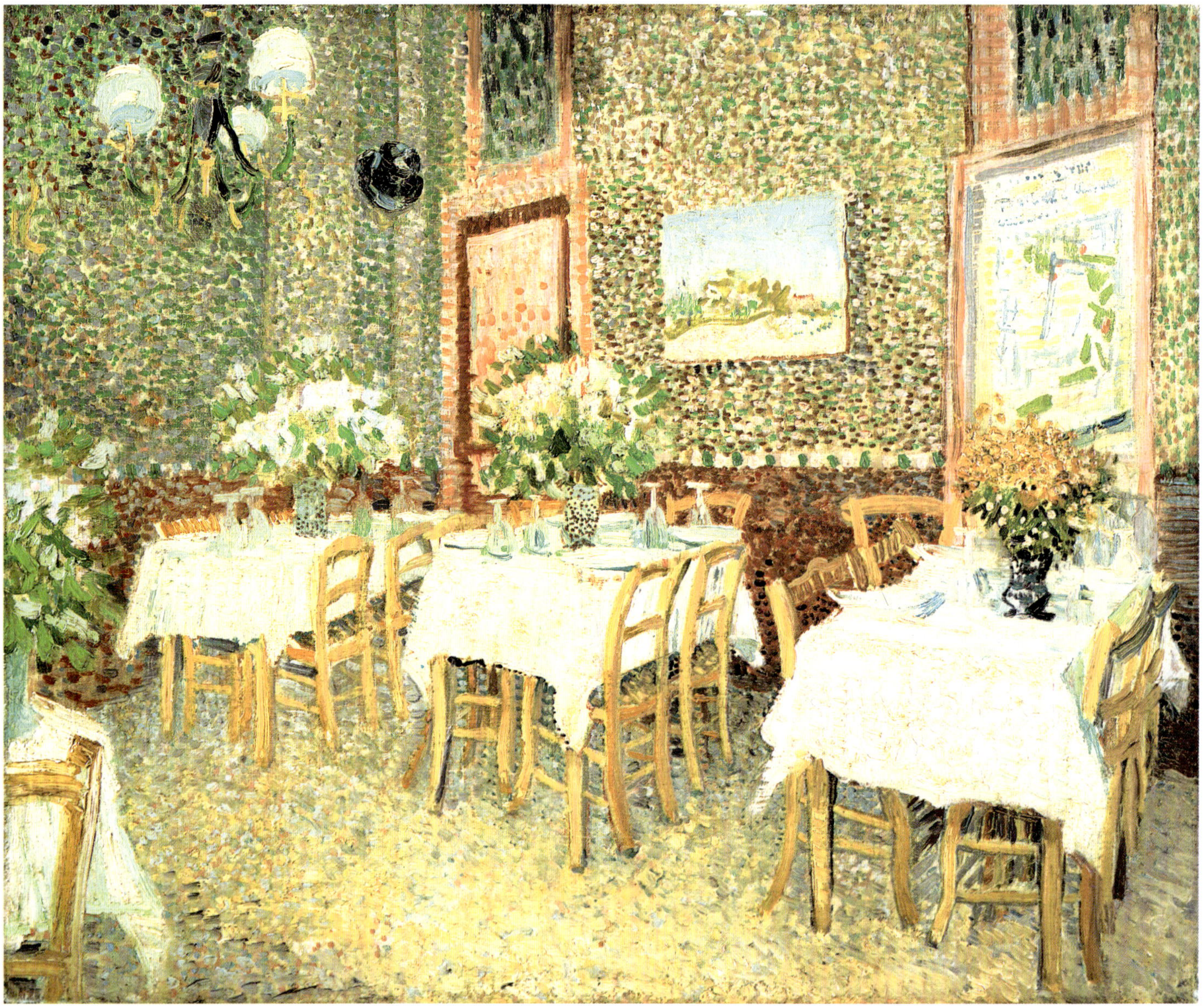

INTERIOR OF A RESTAURANT, Summer 1887
Oil on canvas, 17¾×22 inches (45.5×56.5cm)
Collection State Museum Kröller-Müller, Otterlo

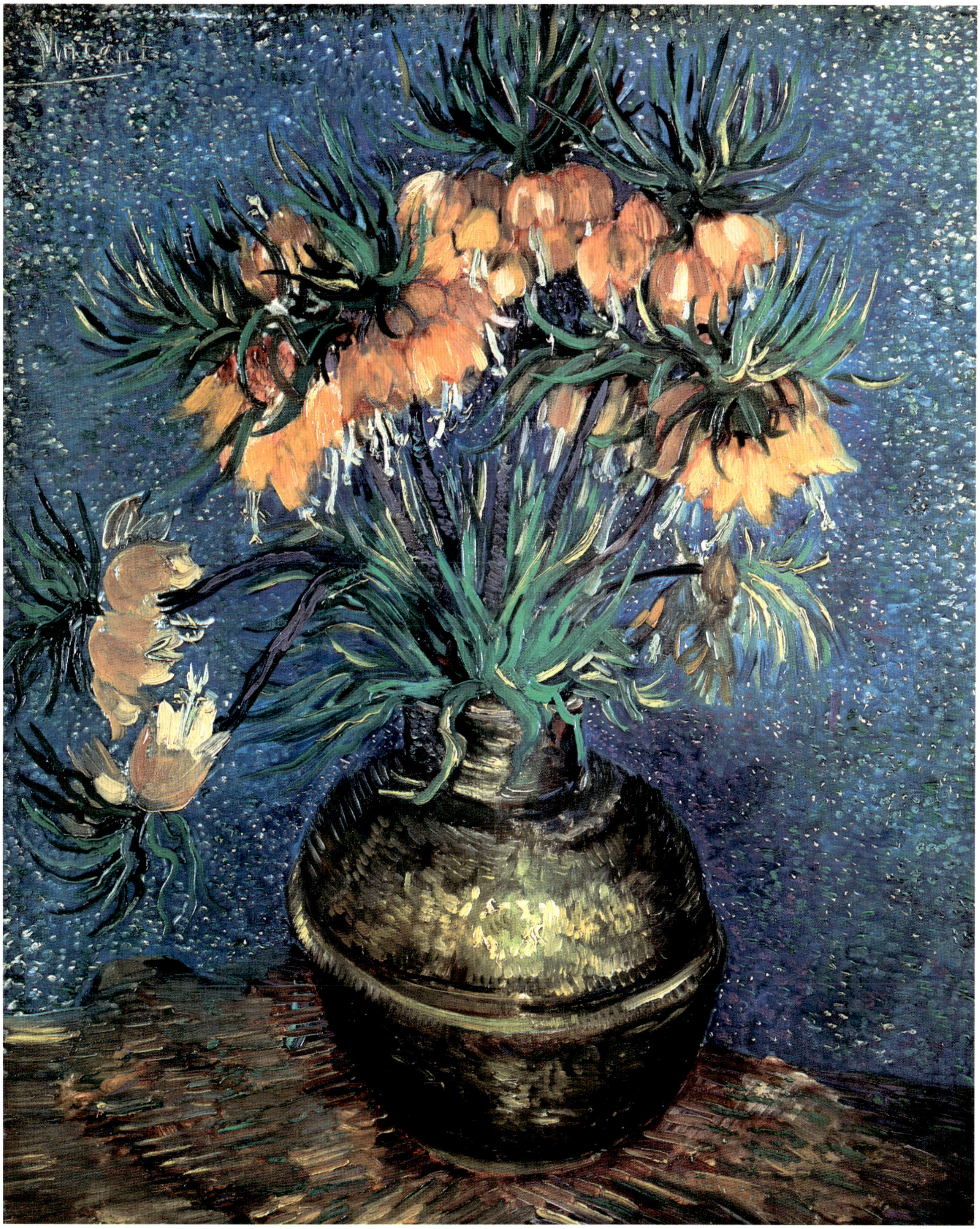

FRITILLARIES IN A COPPER VASE, Summer 1887
Oil on canvas, 29×23¾ inches (73.5×60.5cm)
Musée d'Orsay, Paris

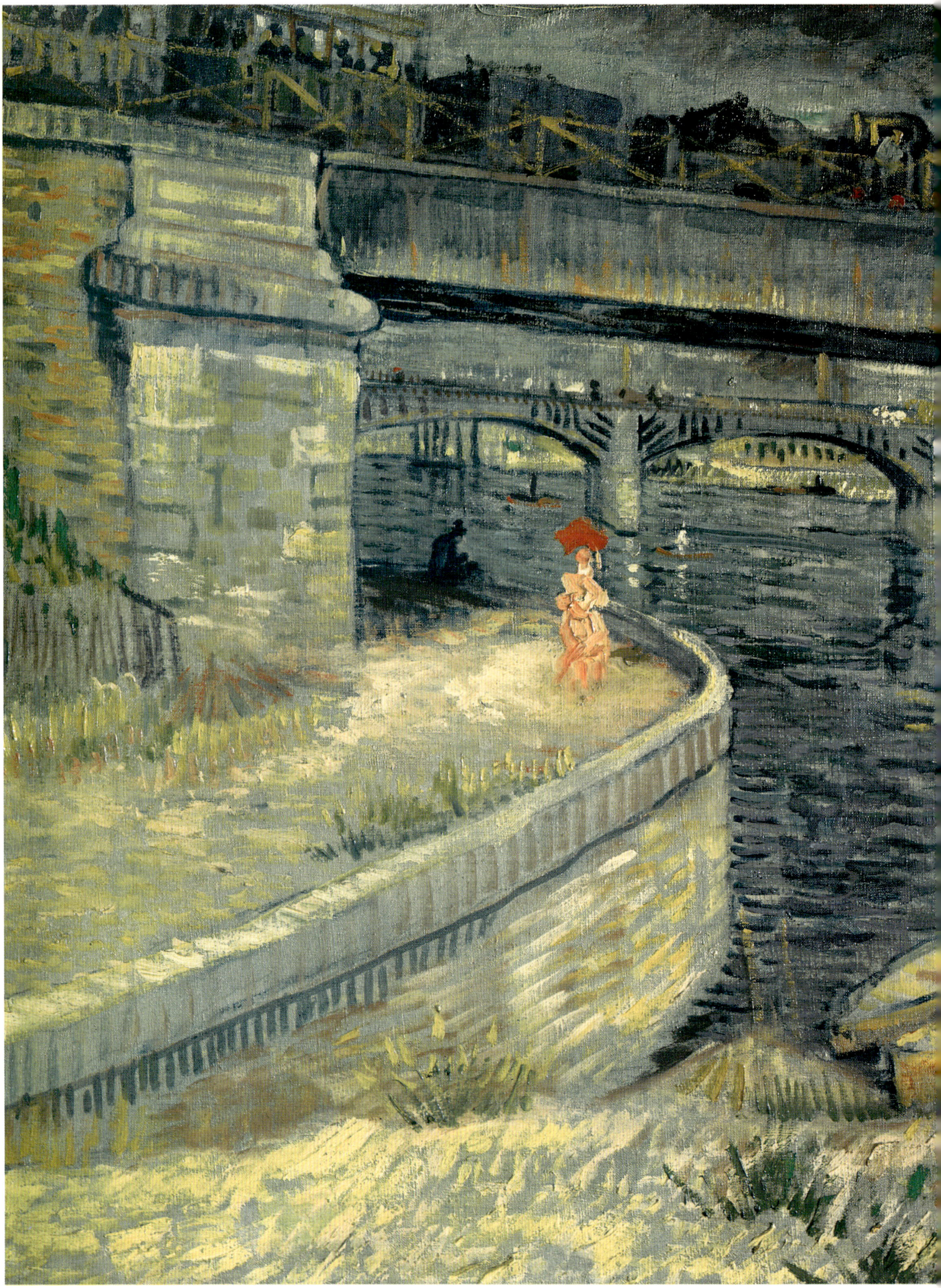

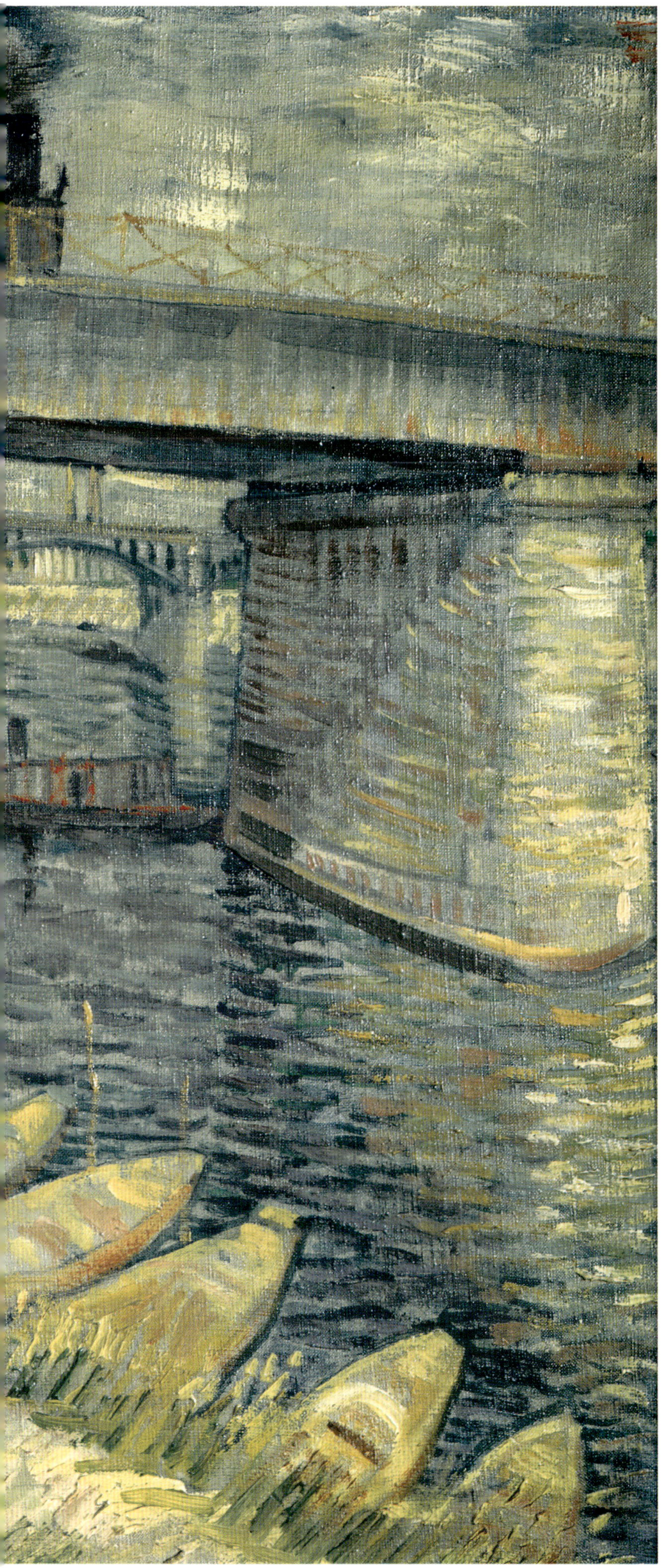

BRIDGE AT ASNIÈRES, July-September 1887
Oil on canvas, 20½×25½ inches (52×65cm)
Stiftung Sammlung E G Bührle, Zurich

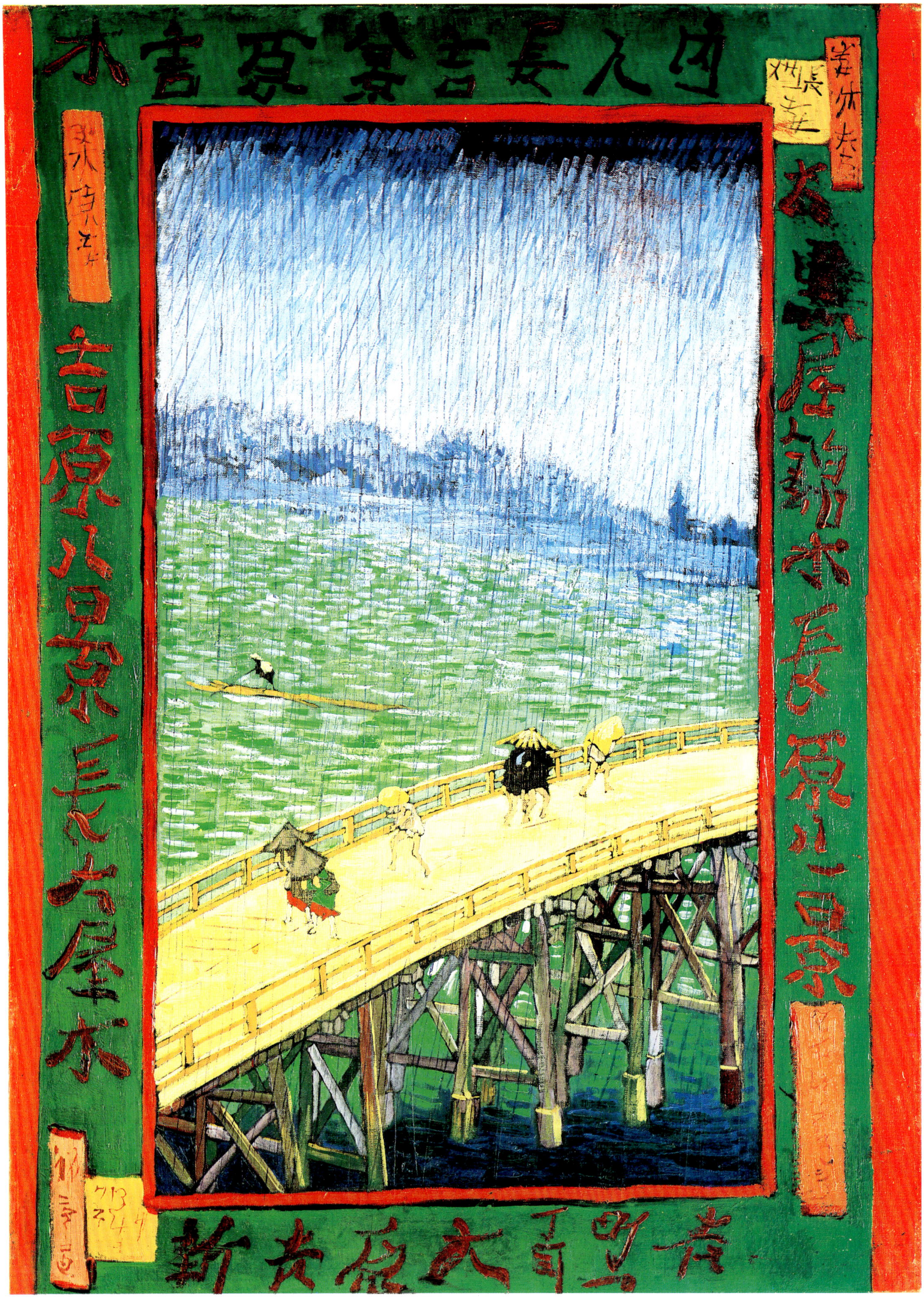

Facing page:
JAPONAISERIE – BRIDGE IN THE RAIN (AFTER HIROSHIGE), Late 1887
Oil on canvas, 28¾×21¼ inches (73×54cm)
Rijksmuseum Vincent van Gogh, Amsterdam

Below:
THE BRIDGE OF LANGLOIS, March 1888
Oil on canvas, 23×28¾ inches (58.5×73cm)
Rijksmuseum Vincent van Gogh, Amsterdam

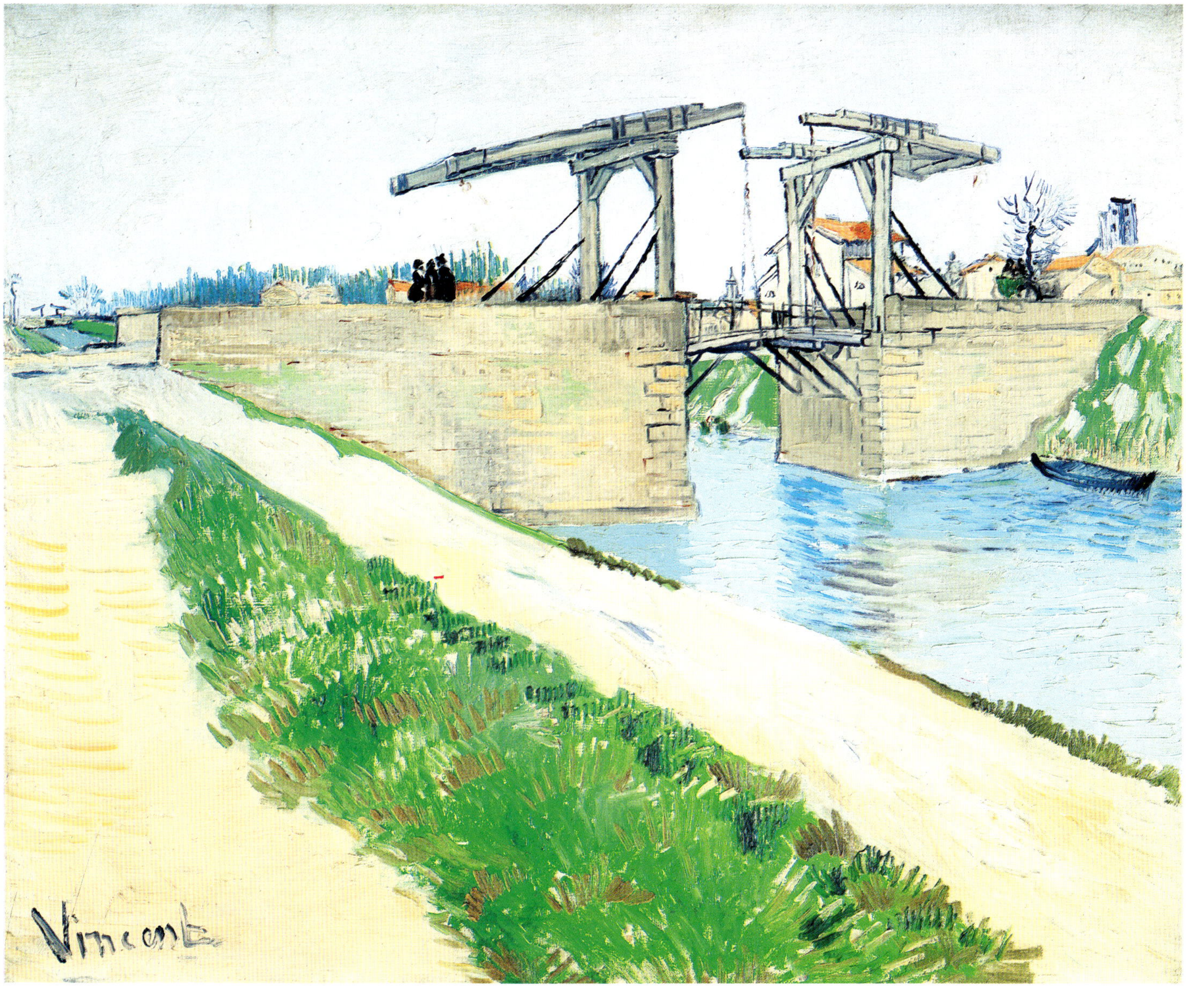

Landscape with the Plains of the Crau,
June 1888
Oil on canvas, 28½×32¼ inches (72.5×92cm)
Rijksmuseum Vincent van Gogh, Amsterdam

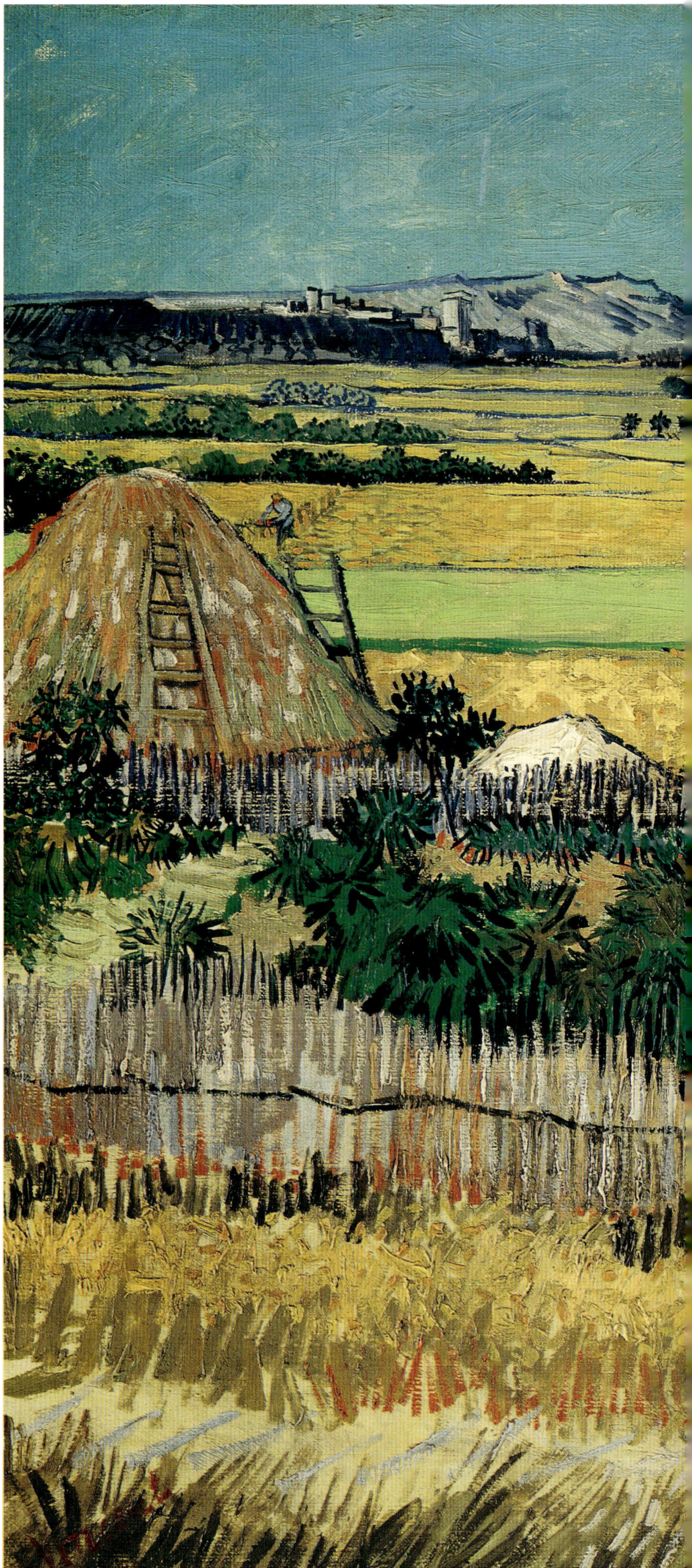

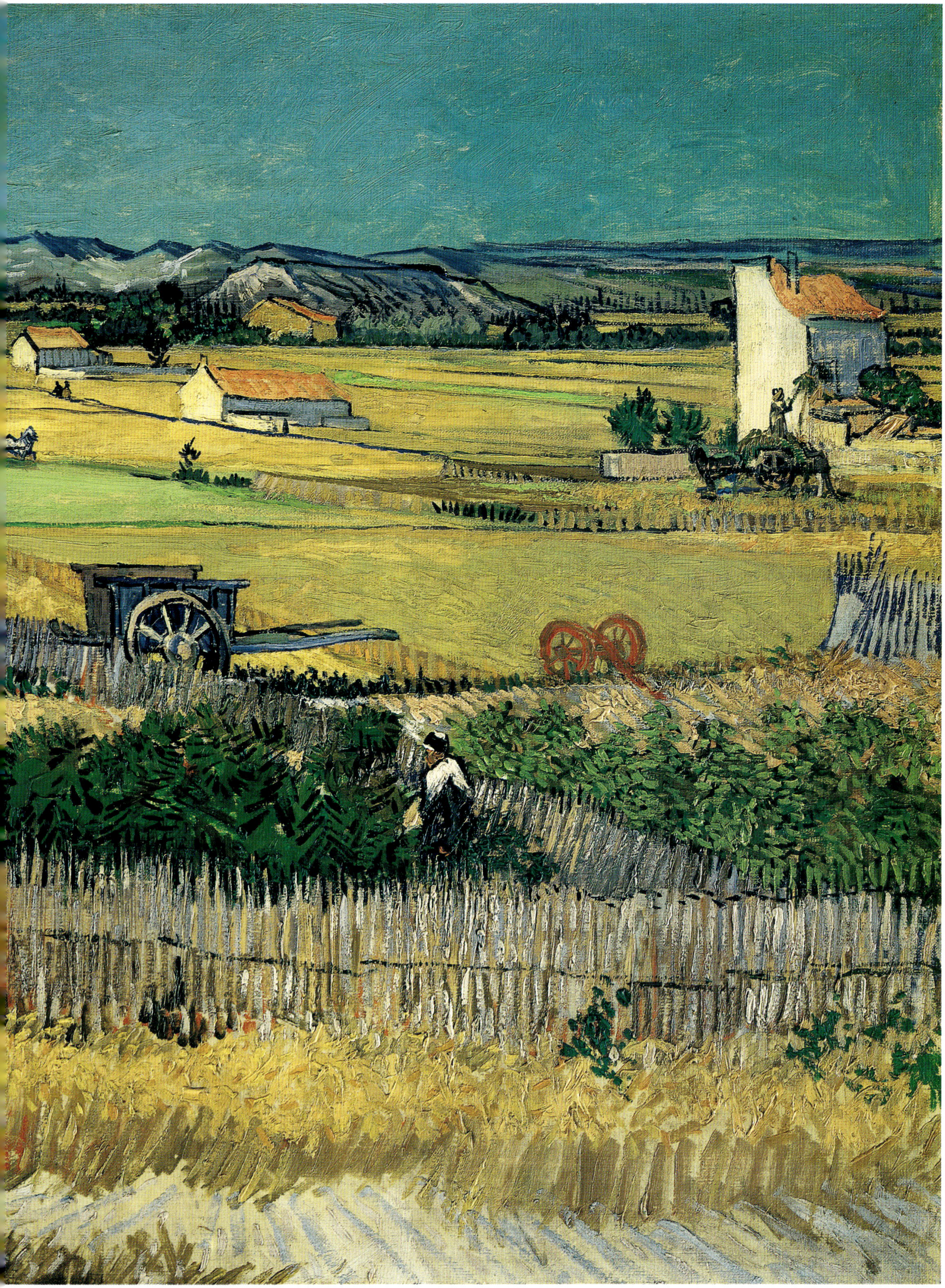

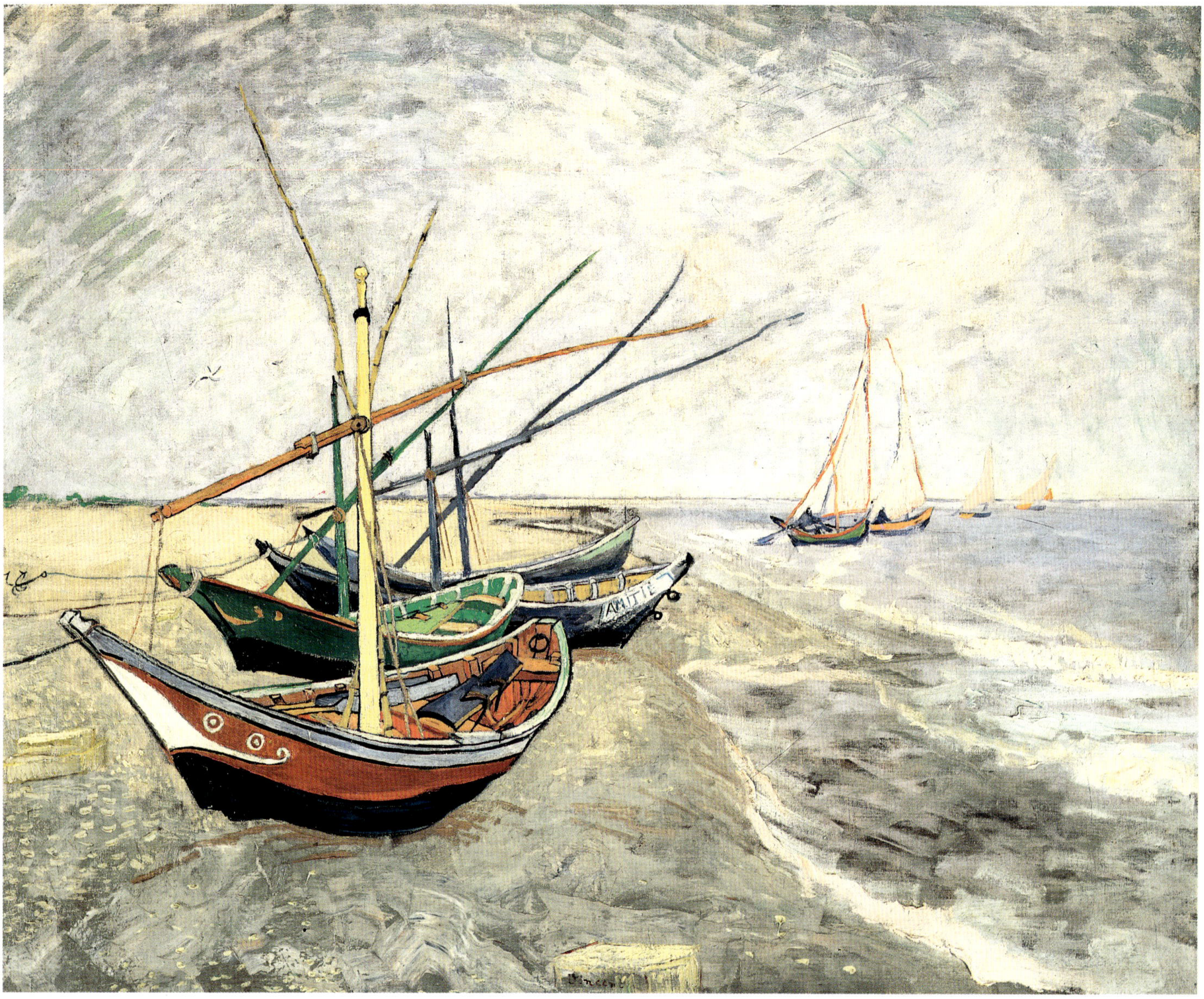

Boats on the Beach at Saintes-Maries, June 1888
Oil on canvas, 25½×31¾ inches (64.5×81cm)
Rijksmuseum Vincent van Gogh, Amsterdam

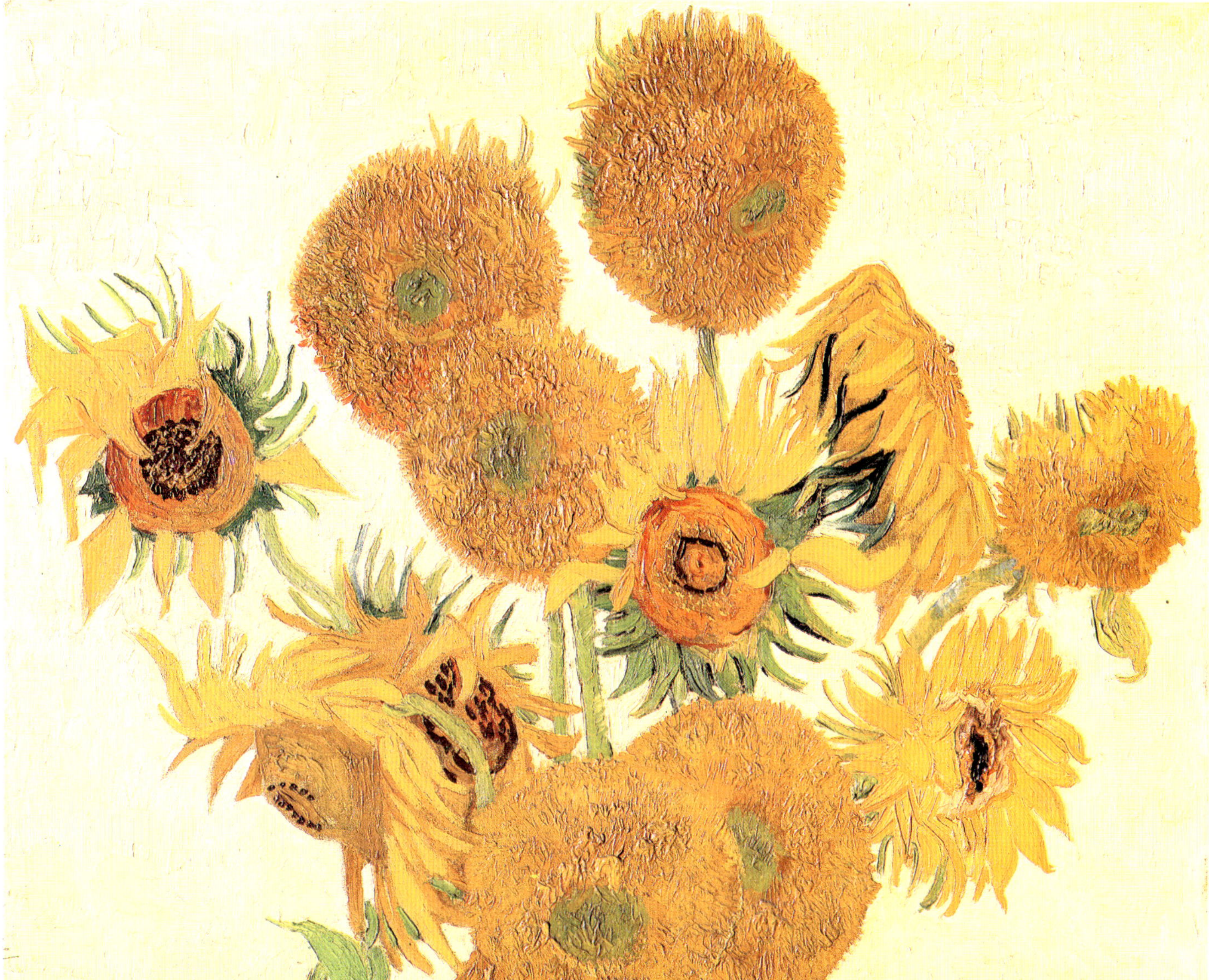

FOURTEEN SUNFLOWERS, August 1888
Oil on canvas, 36½×28¾ inches (93×73cm)
The National Gallery, London

Haystacks in Provence, June 1888
Oil on canvas, 28¾×36¼ inches (73×92.5cm)
Rijksmuseum Kröller-Müller, Otterlo

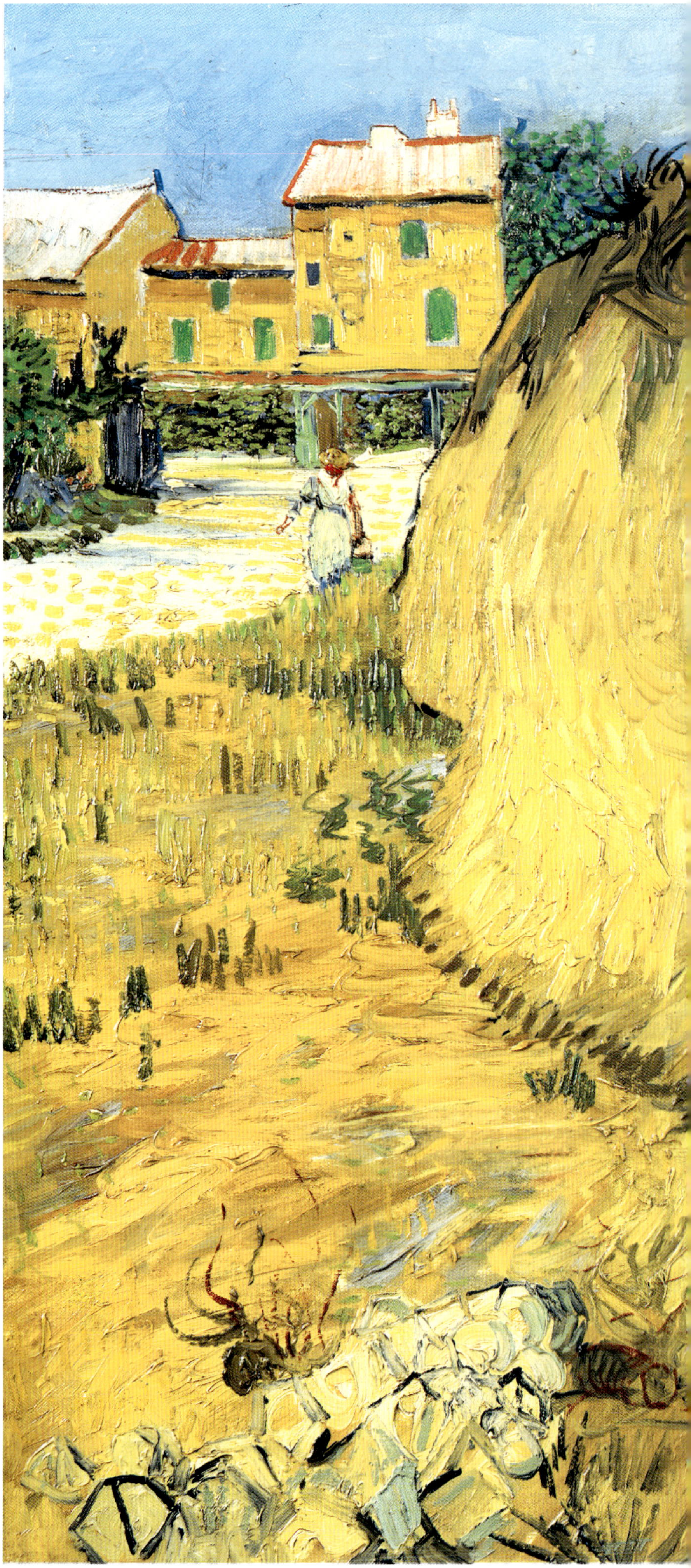

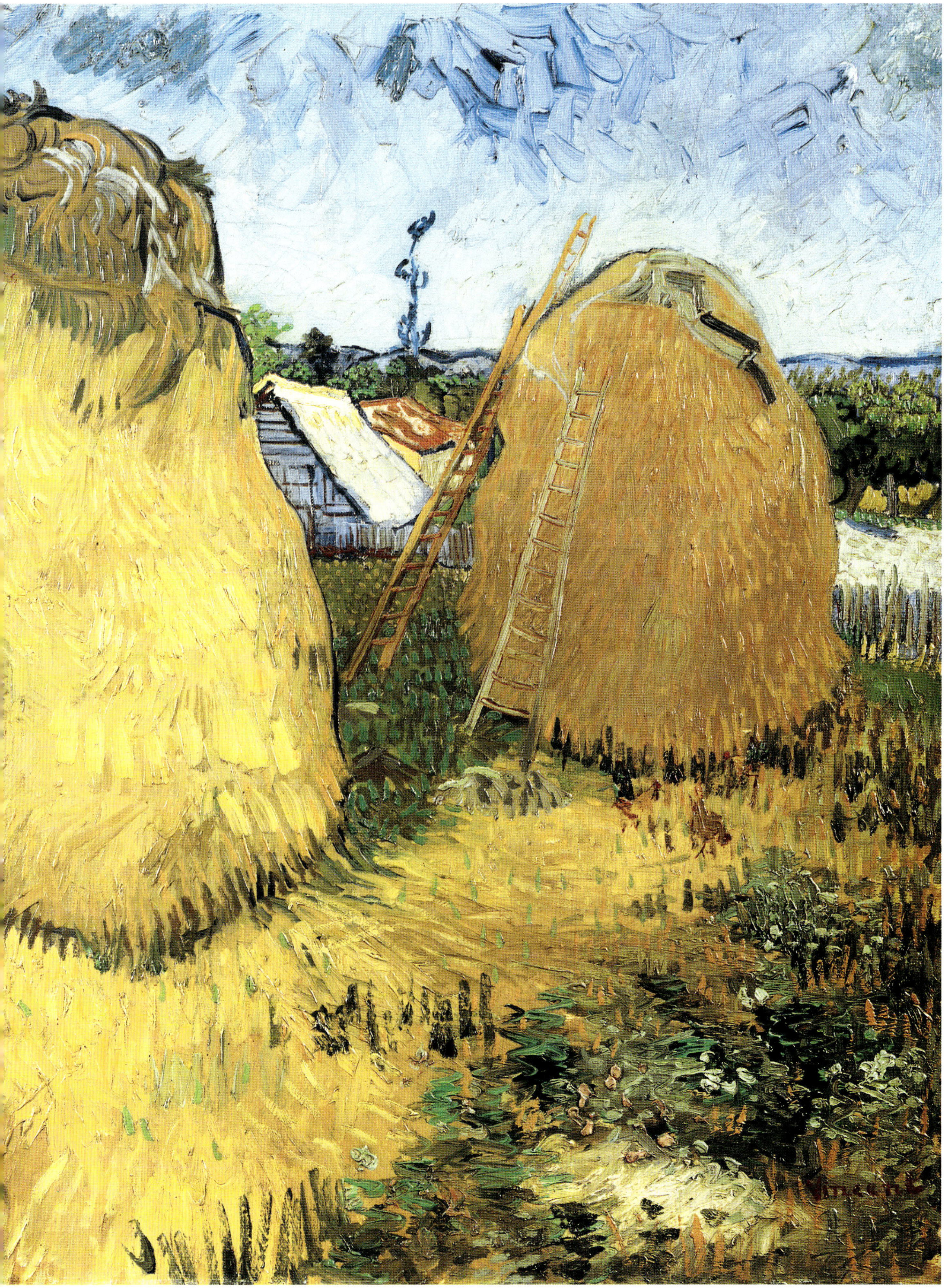
Vincent

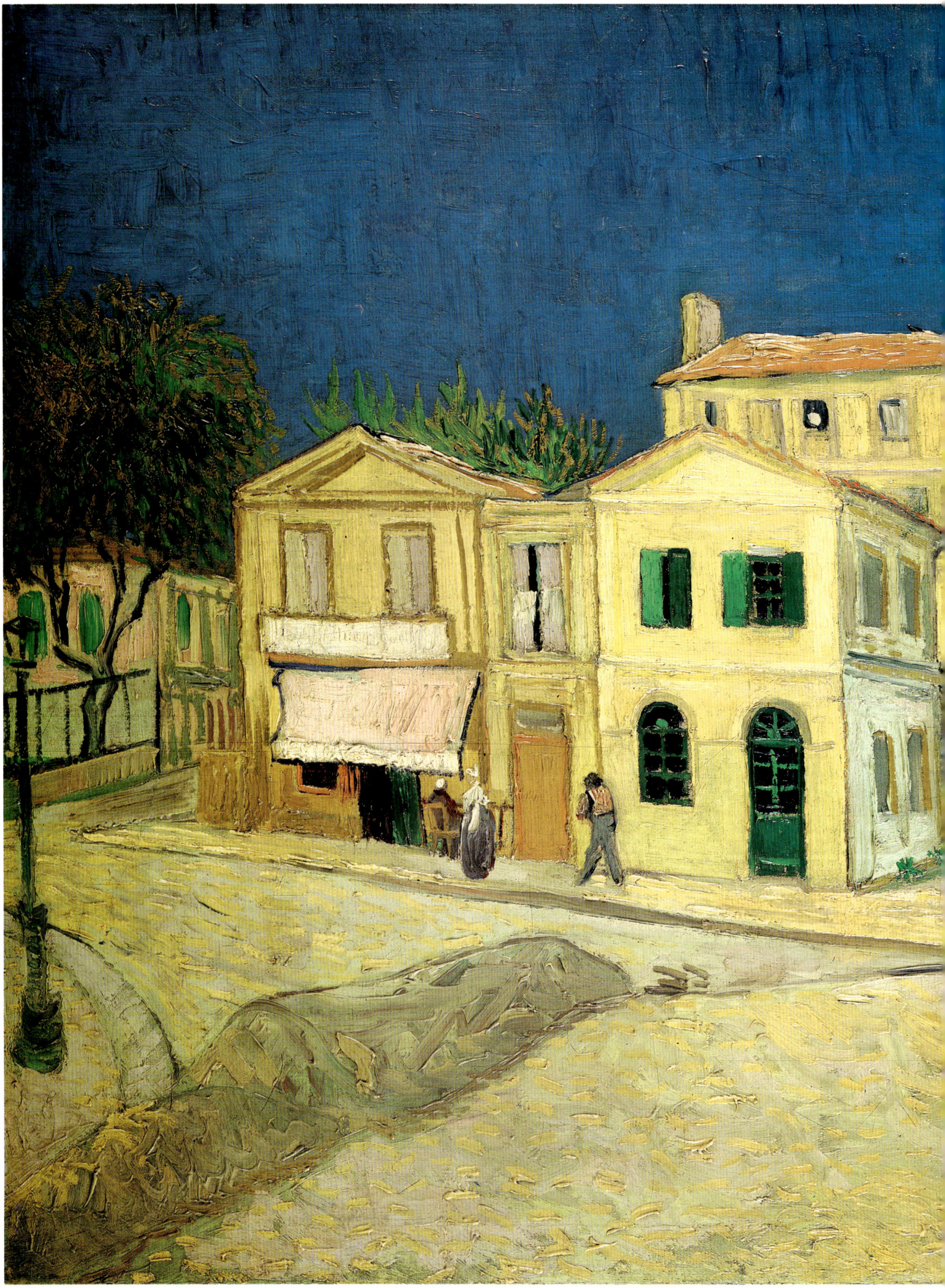

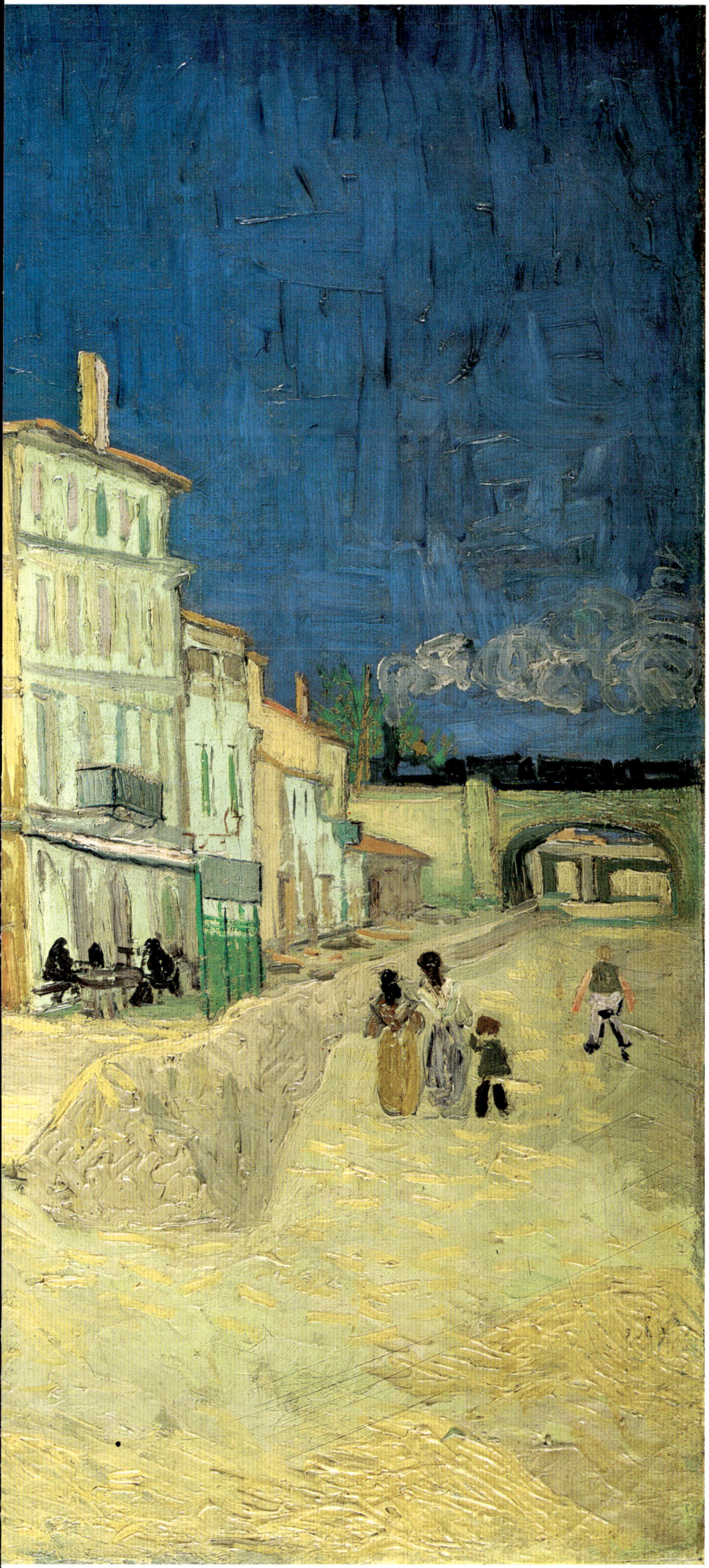

THE YELLOW HOUSE IN ARLES, late September 1888
Oil on canvas, 30×37 inches (76×94cm)
Rijksmuseum Vincent van Gogh, Amsterdam

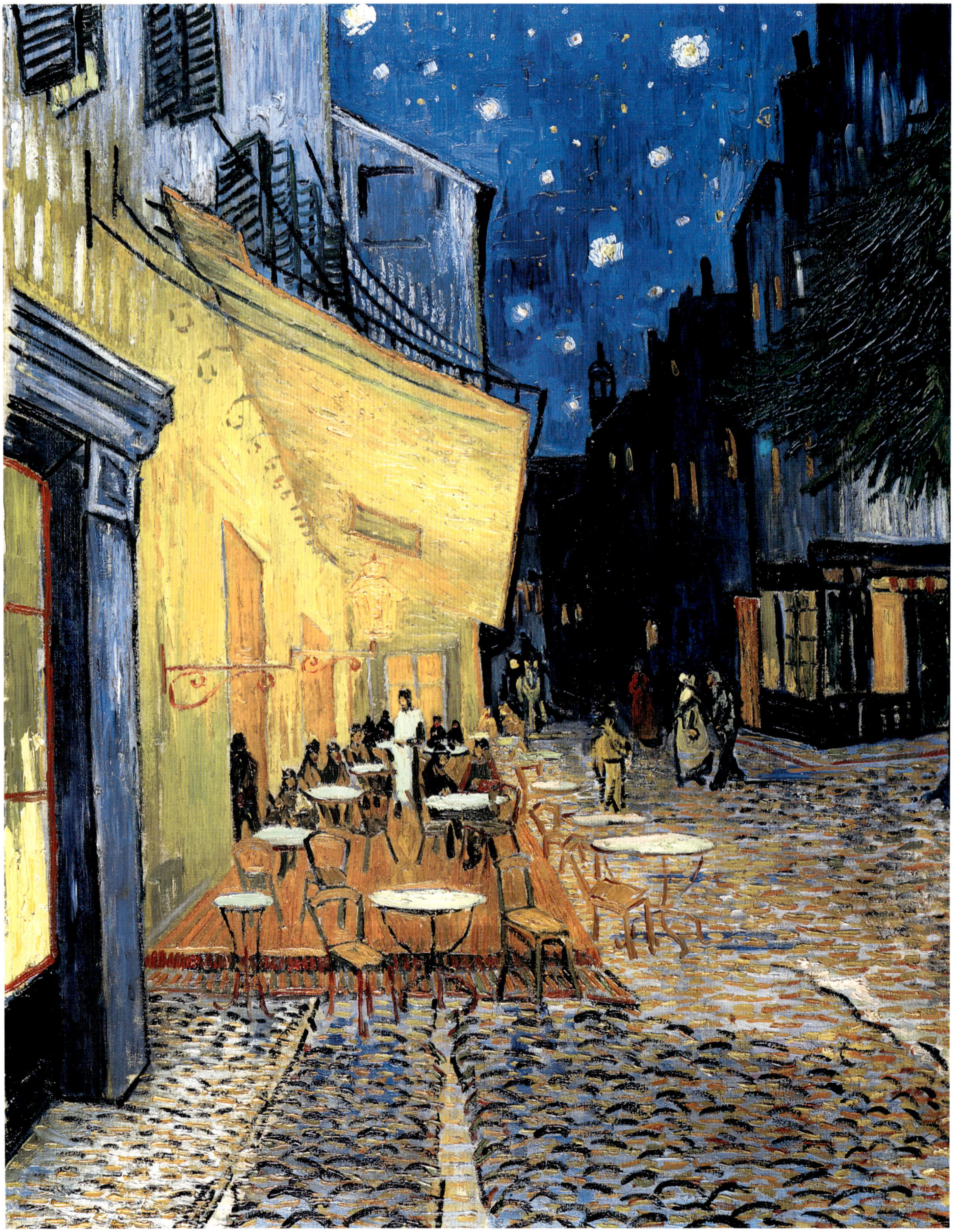

The Café Terrace, Arles at Night, September 1888
Oil on canvas, 32×25¾ inches (81×65.5cm)
Rijksmuseum Kröller-Müller, Otterlo

VAN GOGH'S BEDROOM, MAISON JAUNE, October 1888
Oil on canvas, 28¼×35½ inches (72×90cm)
Rijksmuseum Vincent van Gogh, Amsterdam

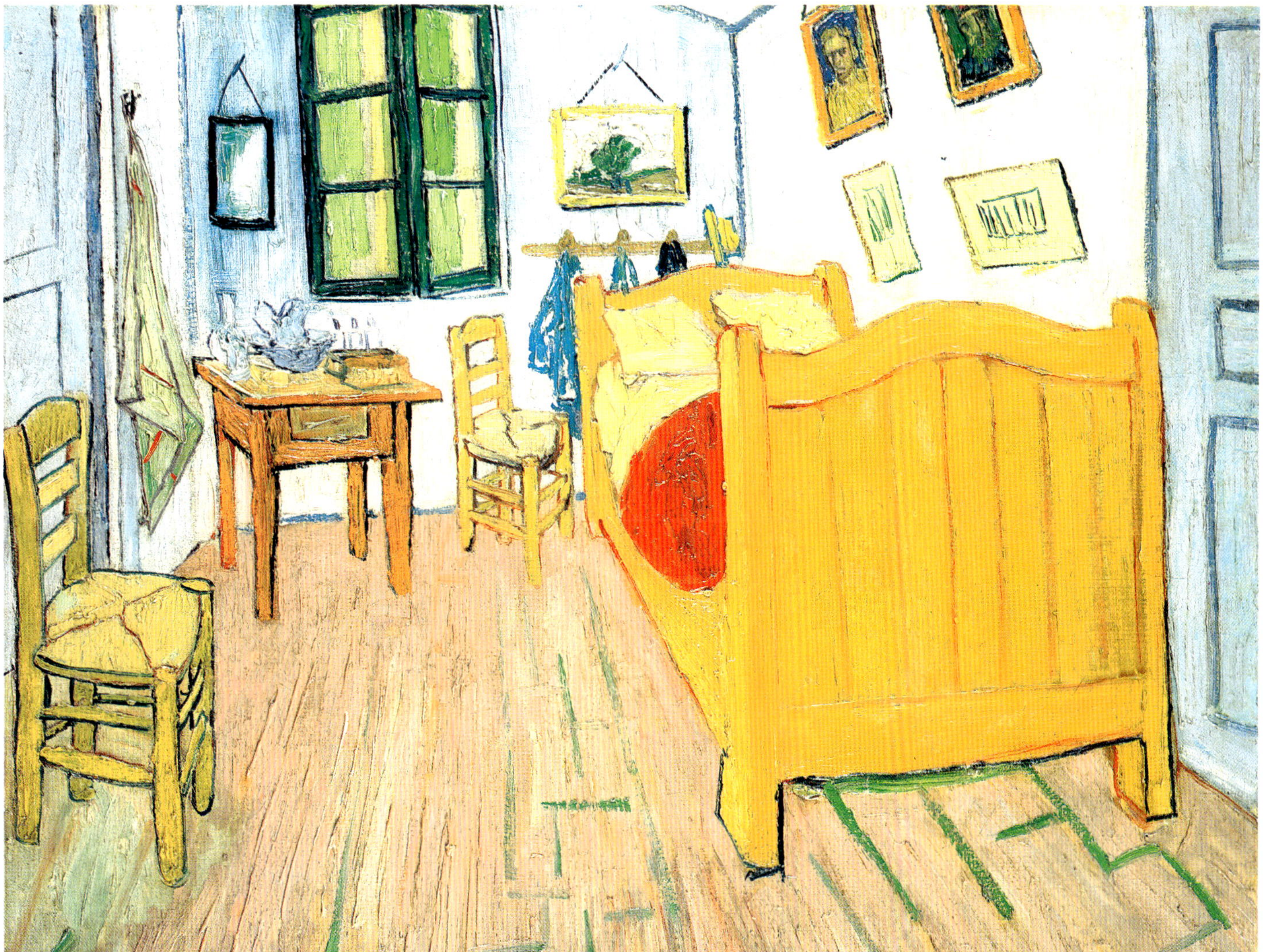

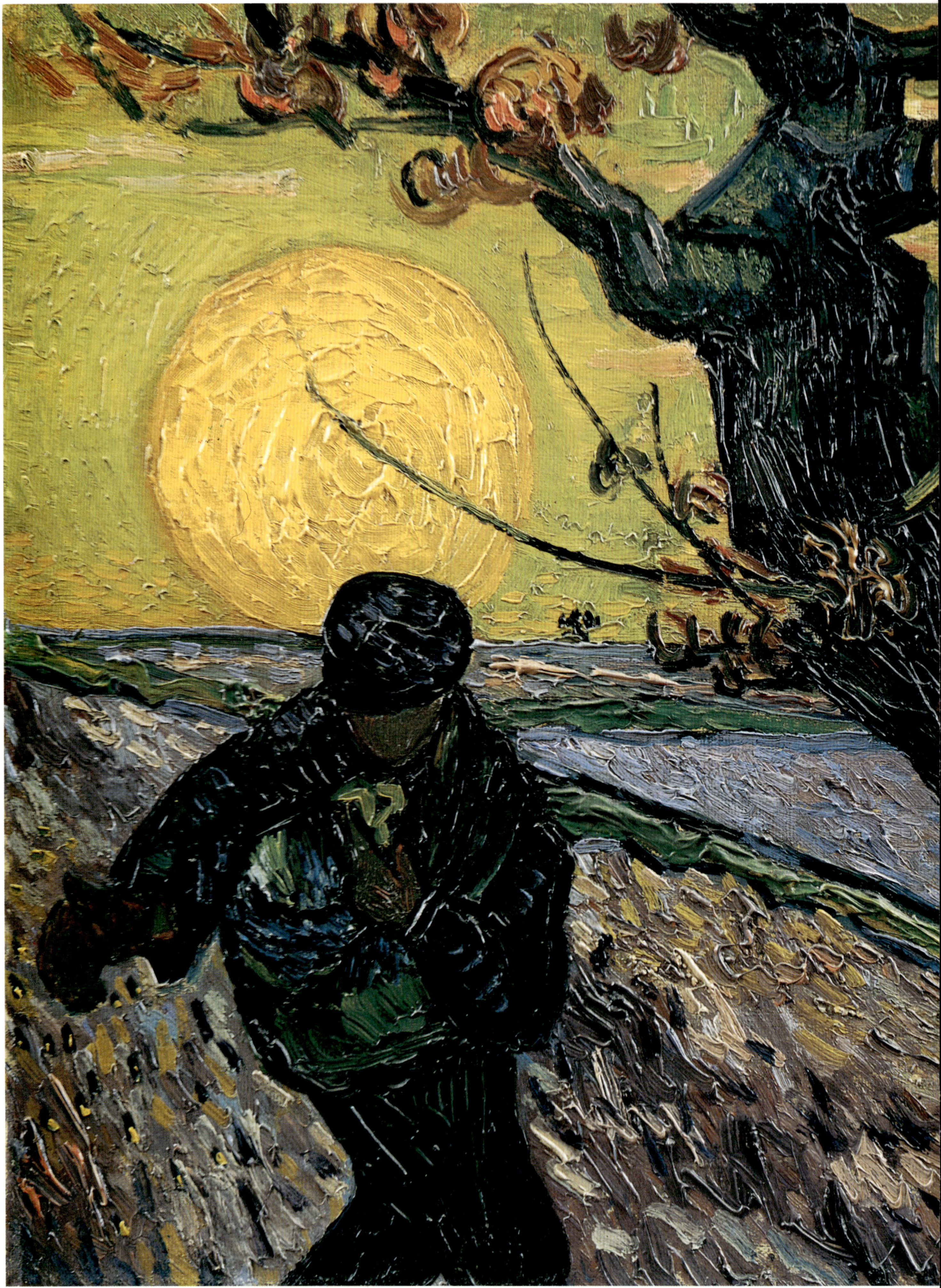

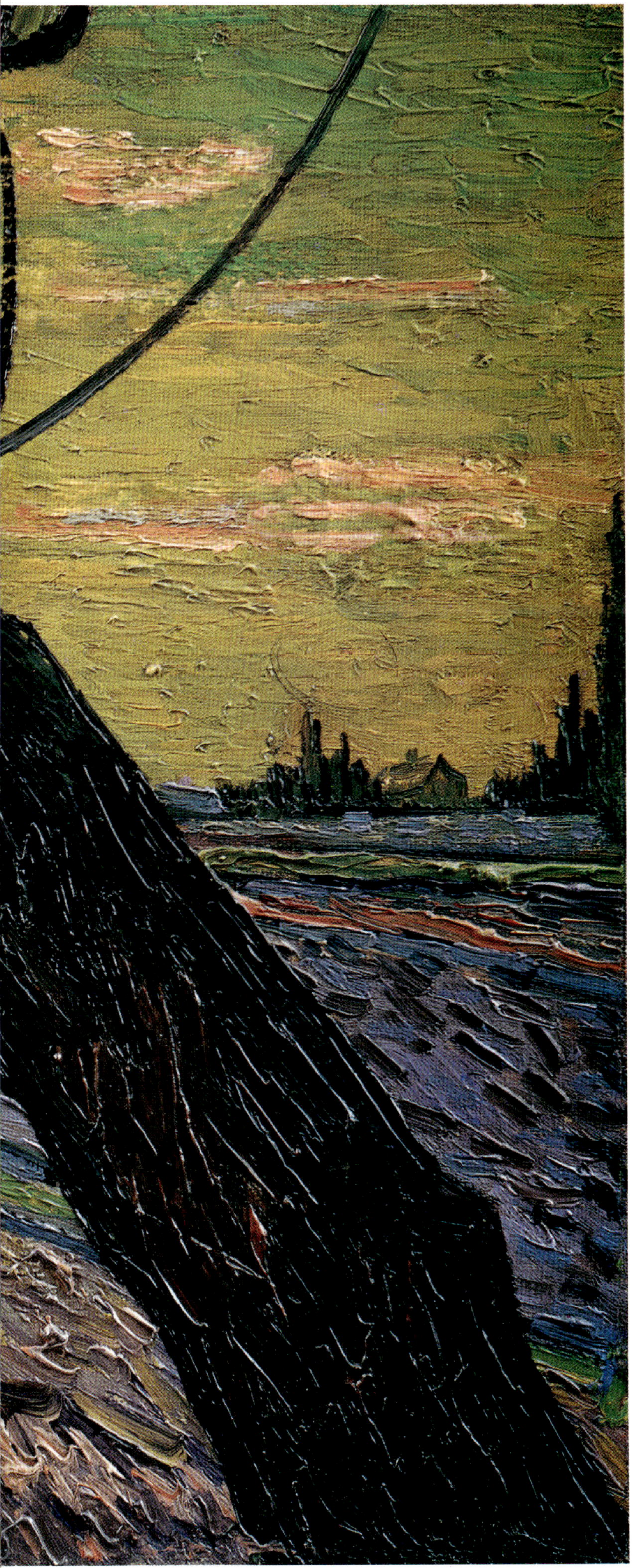

The Sower, November 1888
Oil on canvas, 12½×15¾ inches (32×40cm)
Rijksmuseum Vincent van Gogh, Amsterdam

Irises, 1889
Oil on canvas, 28×37 inches (71×94cm)
J Paul Getty Museum, Malibu

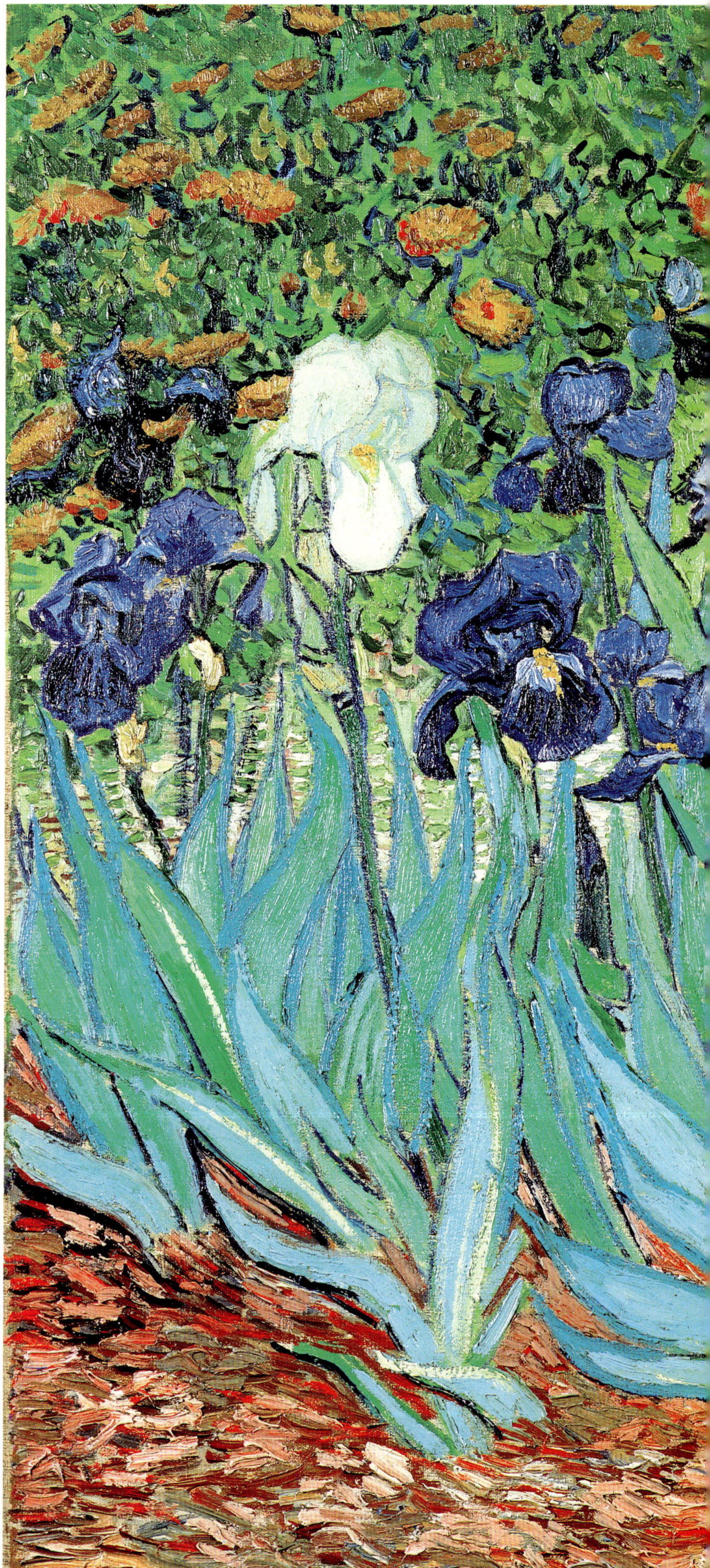

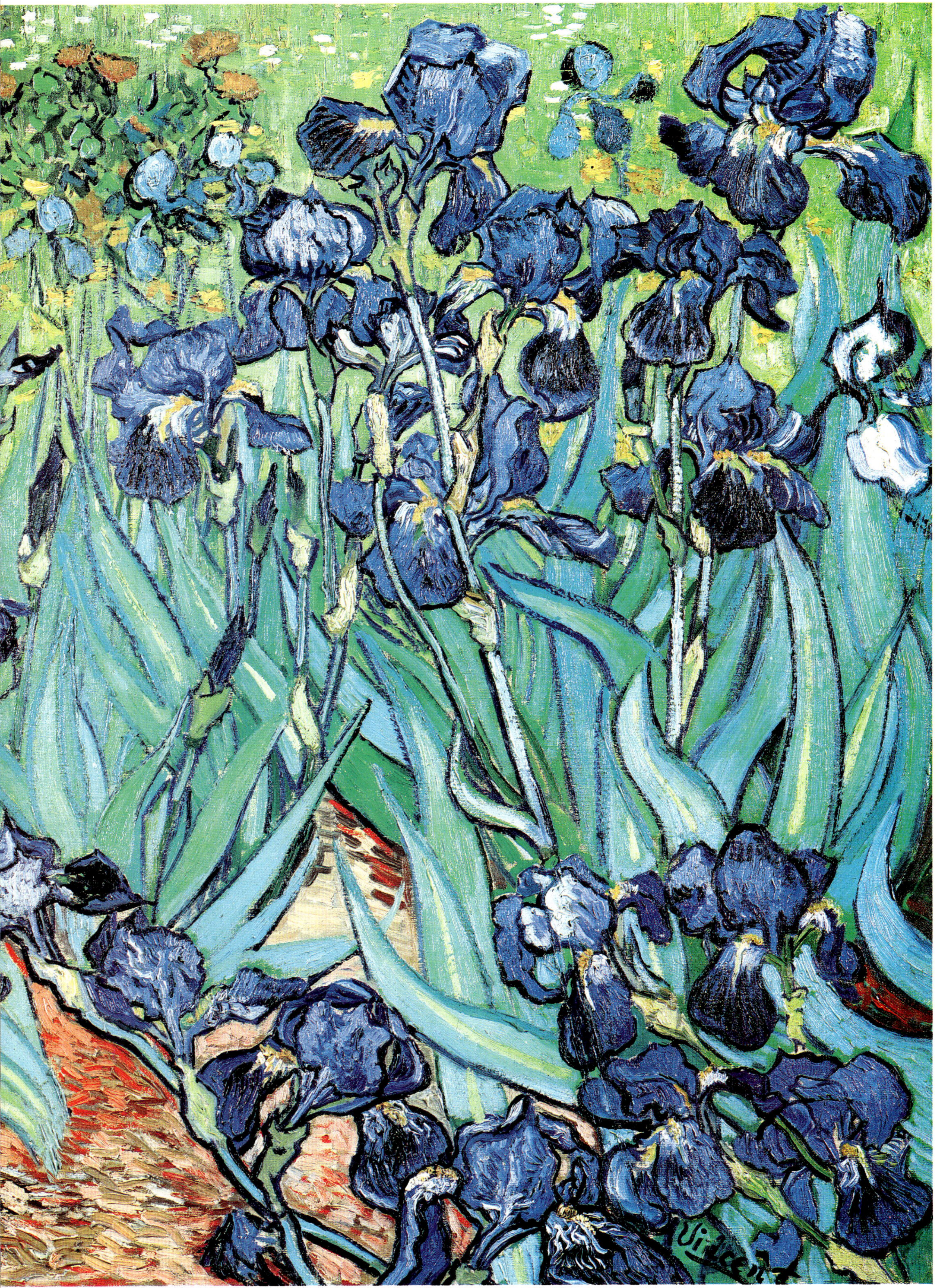
Vincent

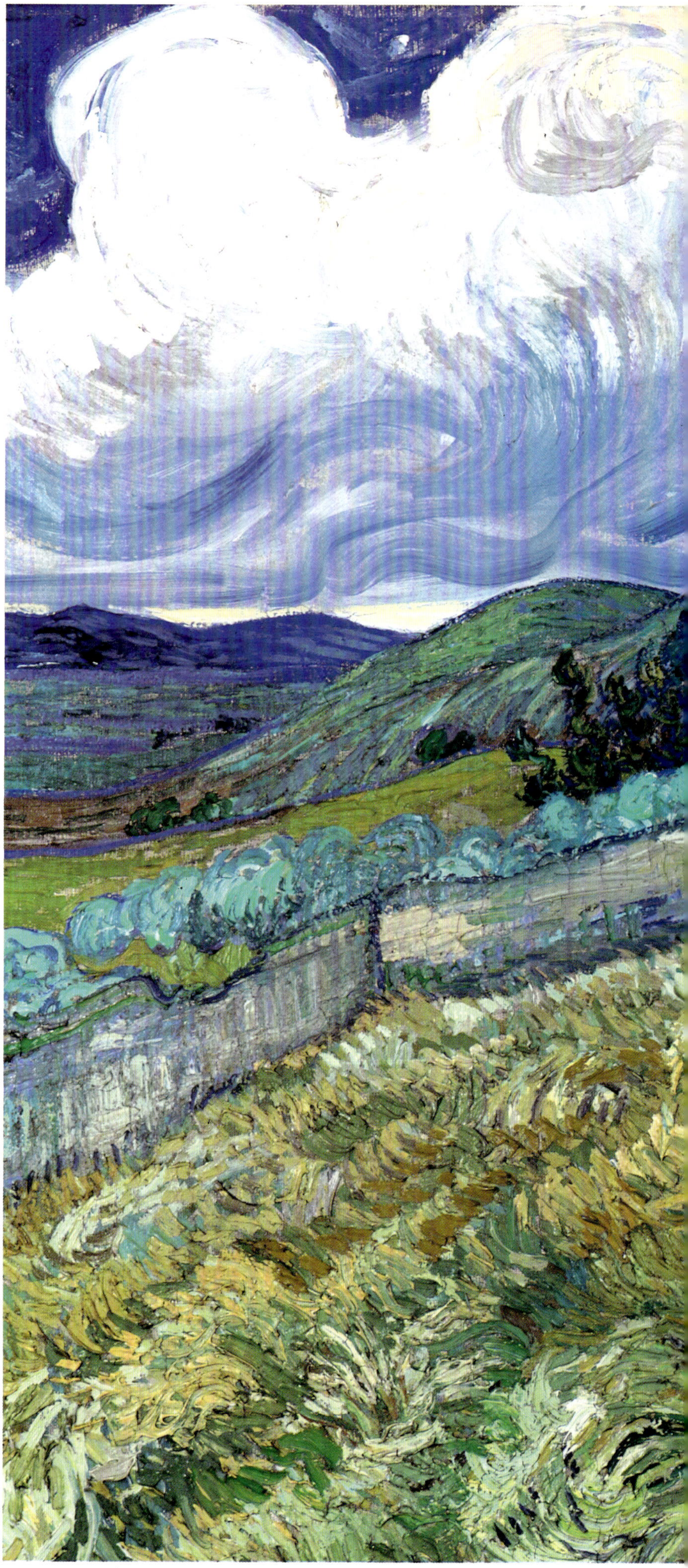

Mountainous Landscape (View from St Paul's Hospital), May 1889
Oil on canvas, 27½×34½ inches (70.5×88.5cm)
Ny Carlsberg Glyptotek, Copenhagen

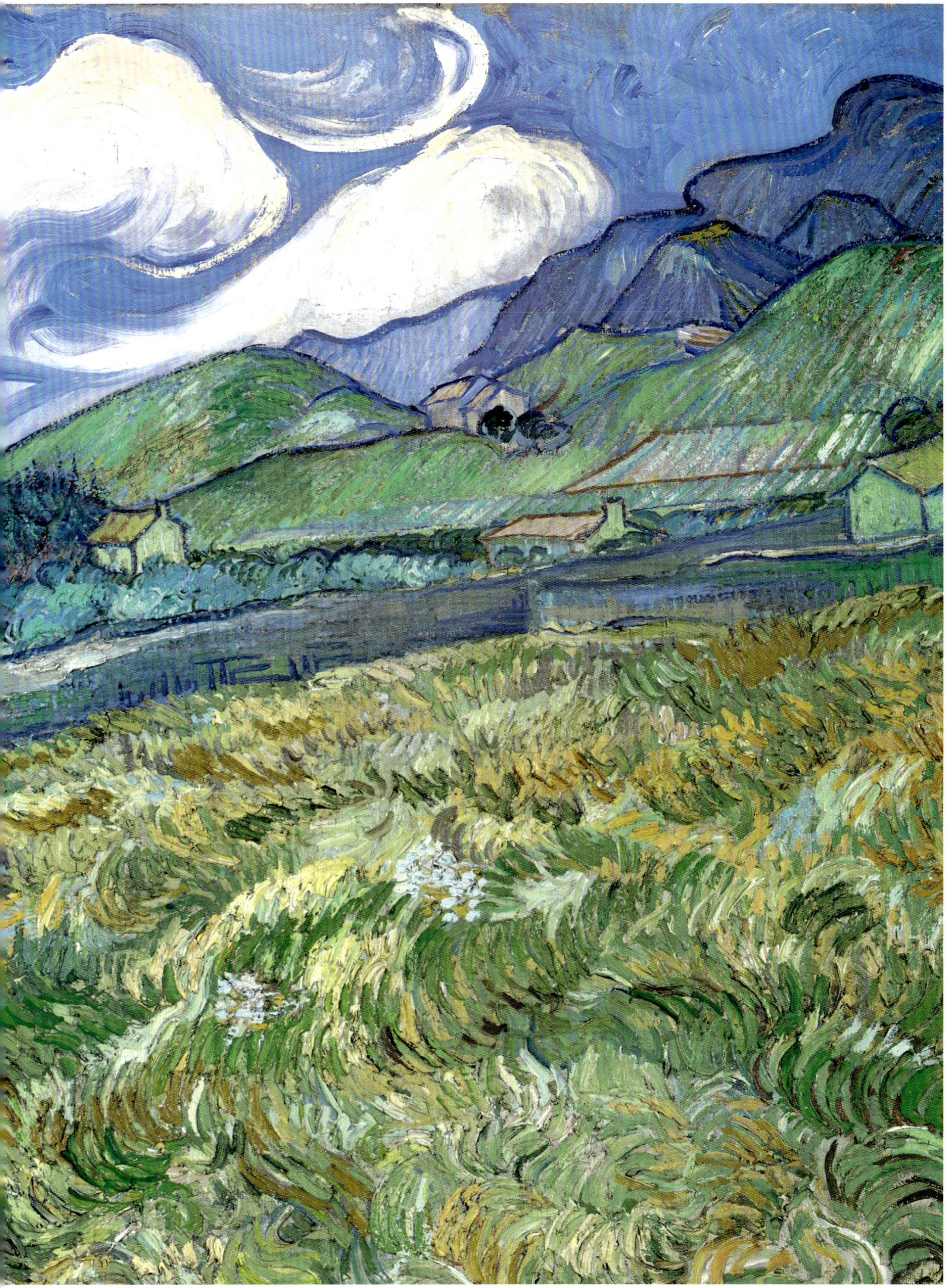

THE STARRY NIGHT, June 1889
Oil on canvas, 29×36¼ inches (73.7×92.1cm)
The collection of the Museum of Modern Art, New York

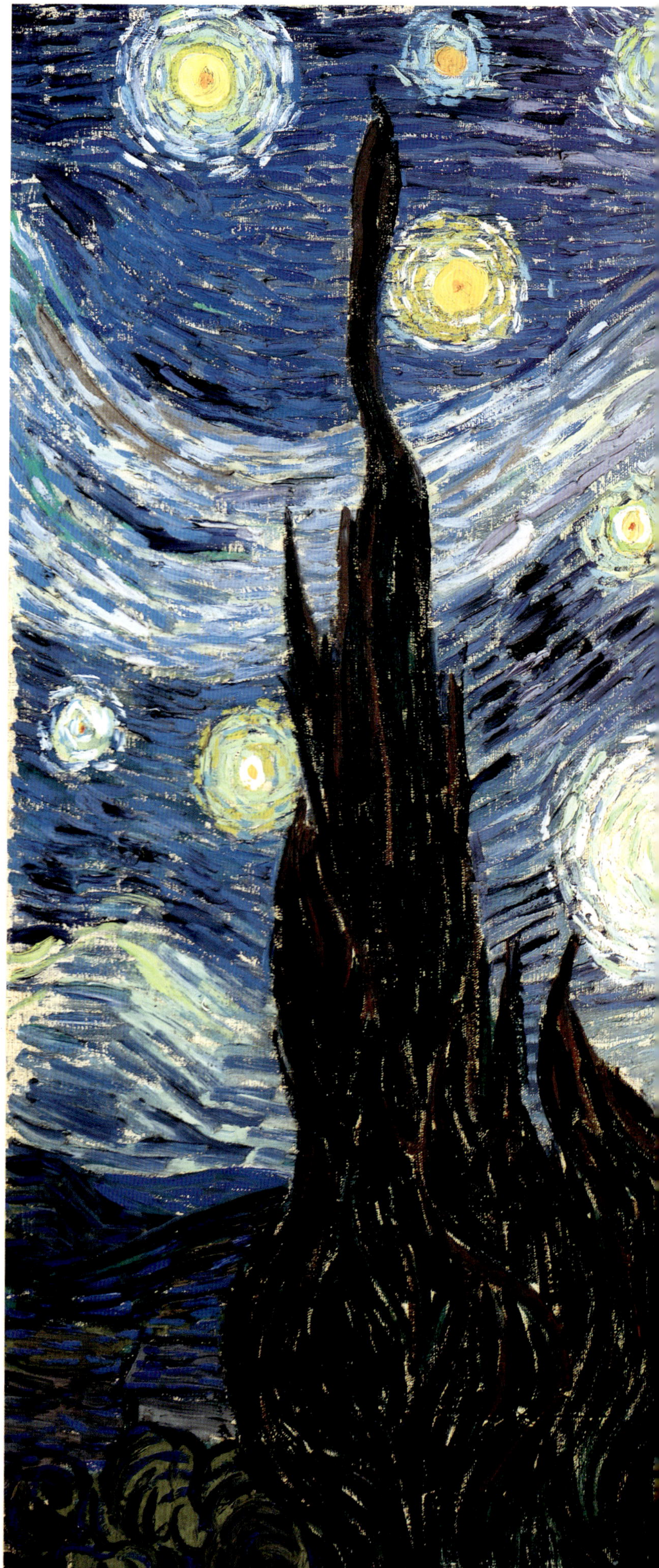

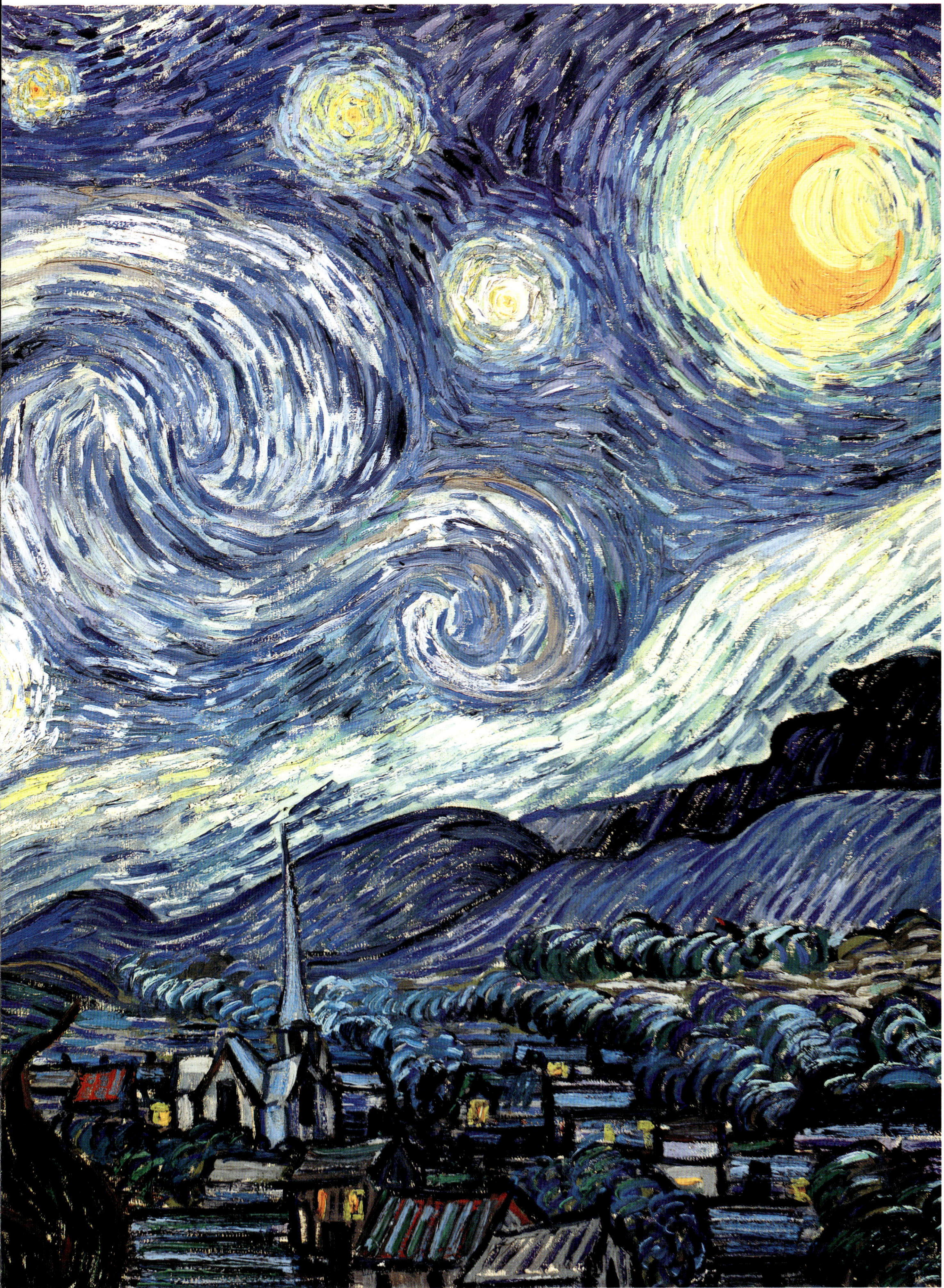

Pietà (after Delacroix), September 1889
Oil on canvas, 28¾×23¾ inches (73×60.5cm)
Rijksmuseum Vincent van Gogh, Amsterdam

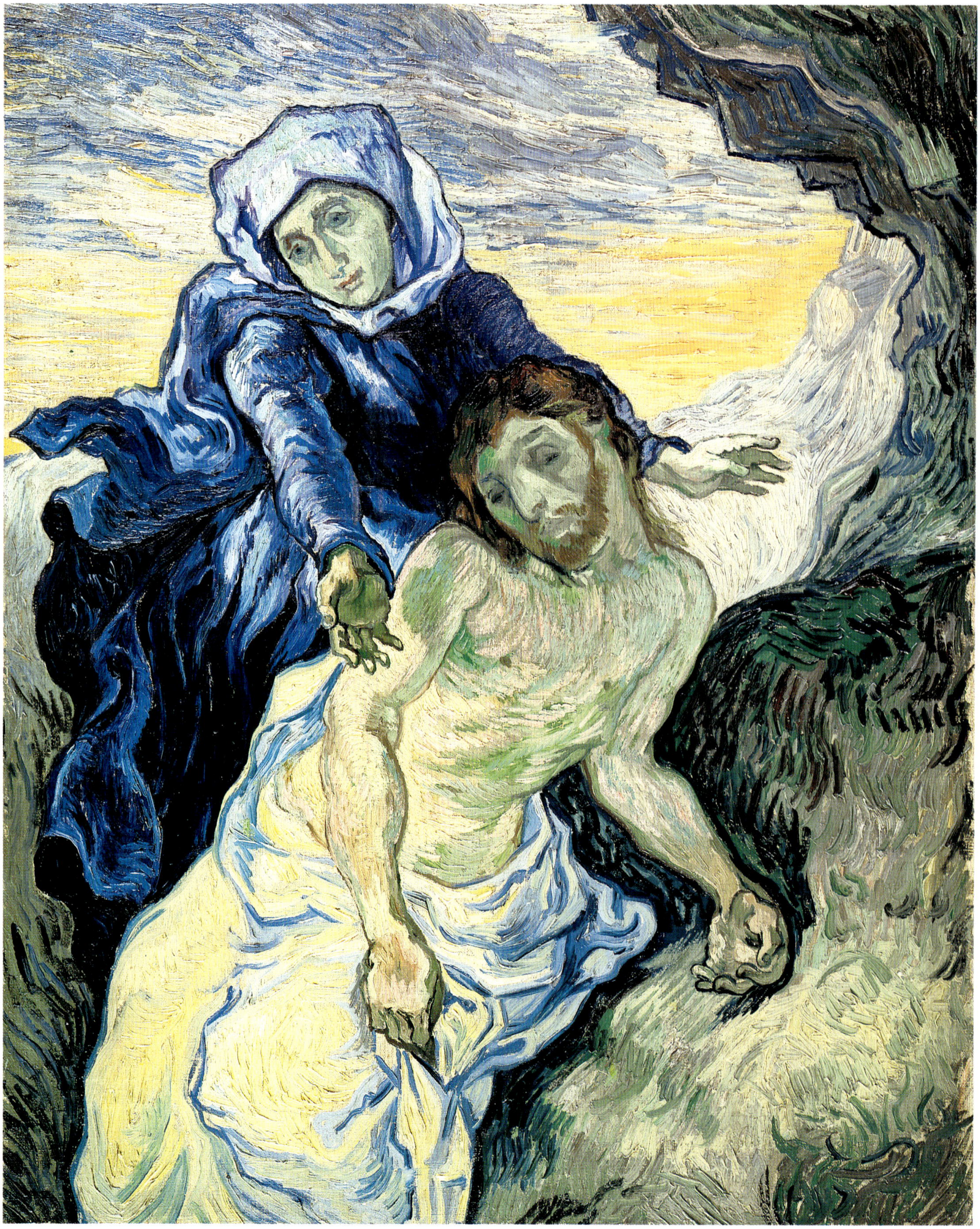

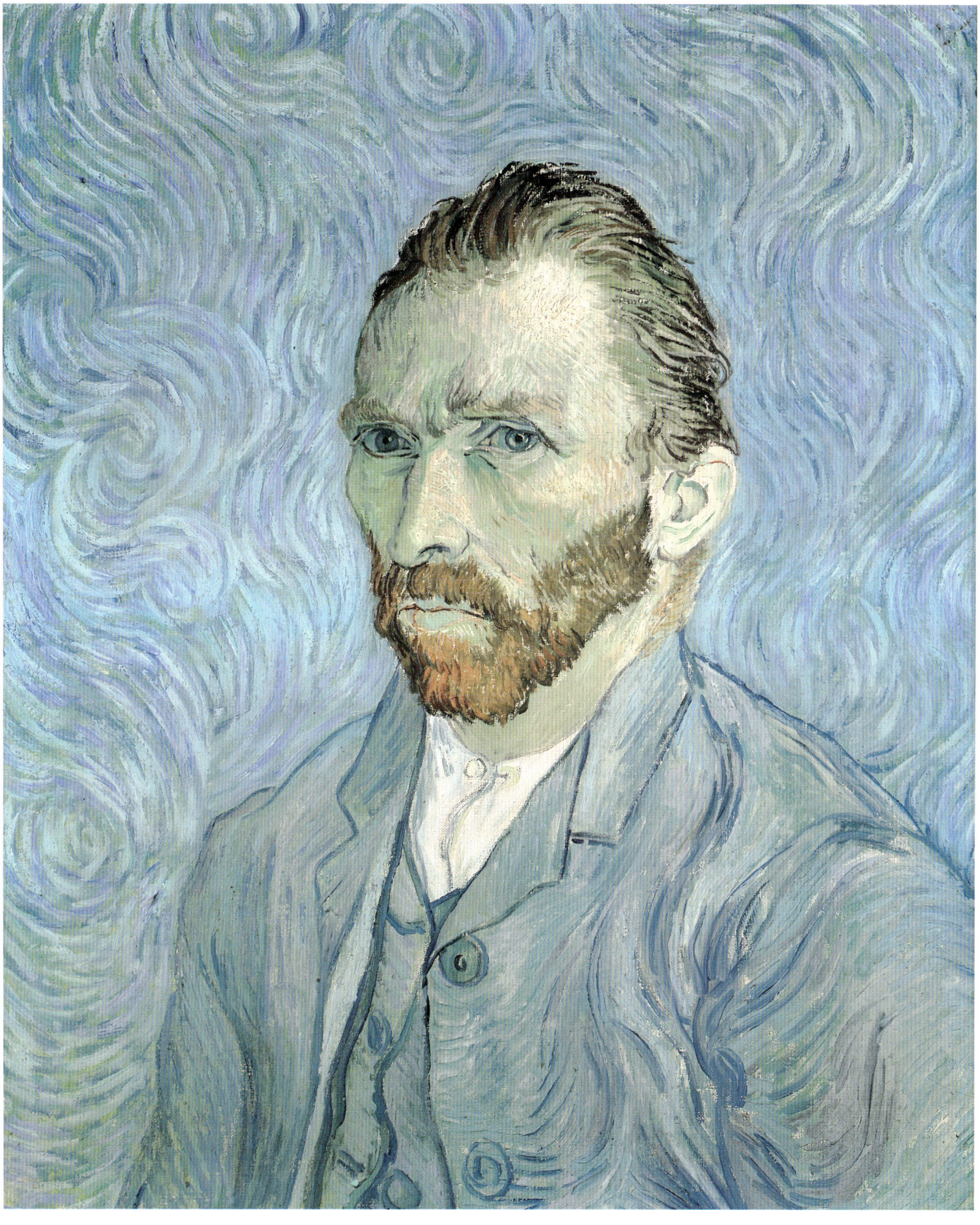

Self-Portrait, September 1889
Oil on canvas, 25½×21¼ inches (65×54cm)
Musée d'Orsay, Paris

Noon or the Siesta (after Millet),
January 1890
Oil on canvas, 28½×35½ inches (73×91cm)
Musée d'Orsay, Paris

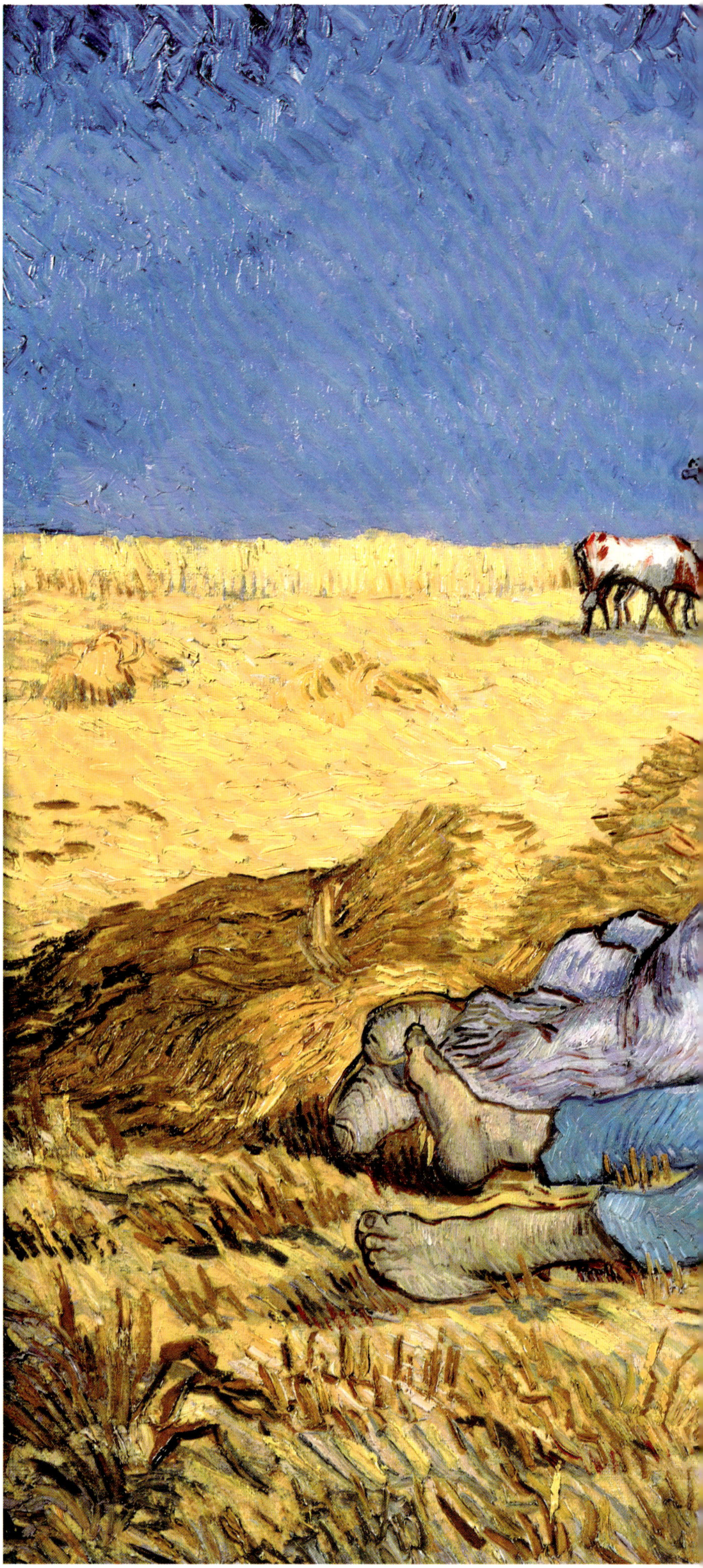

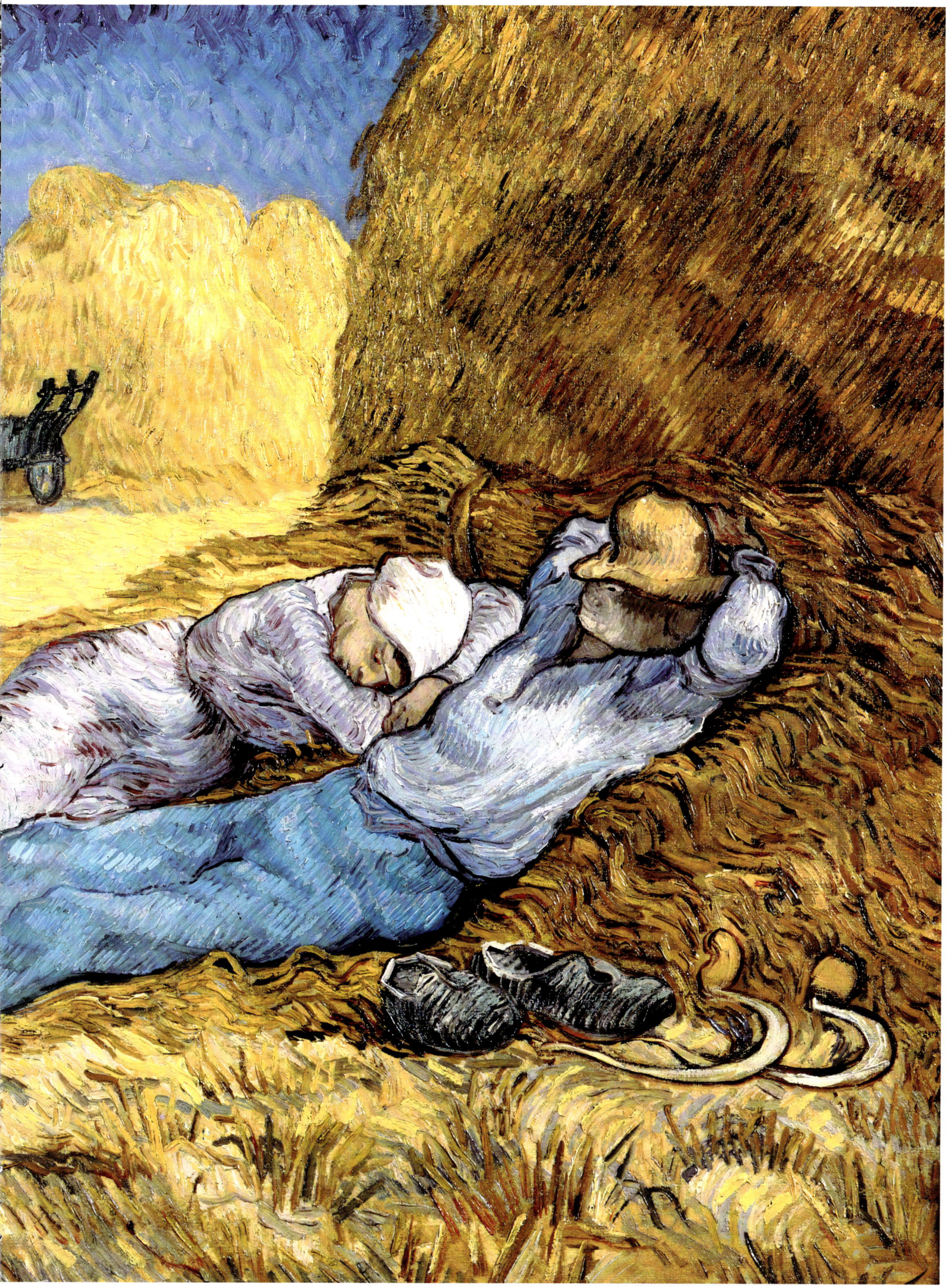

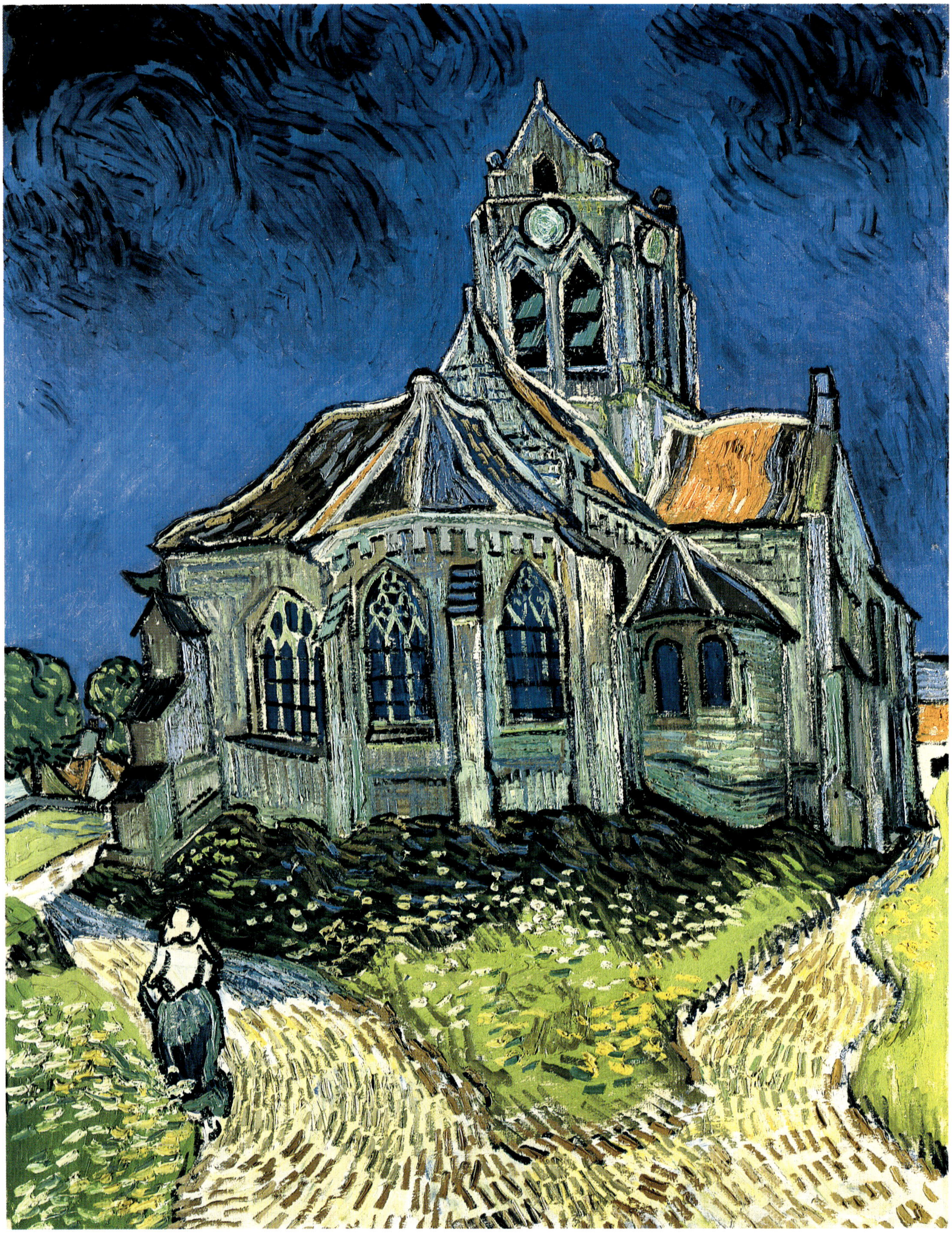

THE CHURCH AT AUVERS, June 1890
Oil on canvas, 37×29¾ inches (94×75.4cm)
Musée d'Orsay, Paris

Dr Paul Gachet, June 1890
Oil on canvas, 26¾×22½ inches (68×57cm)
Musée d'Orsay, Paris

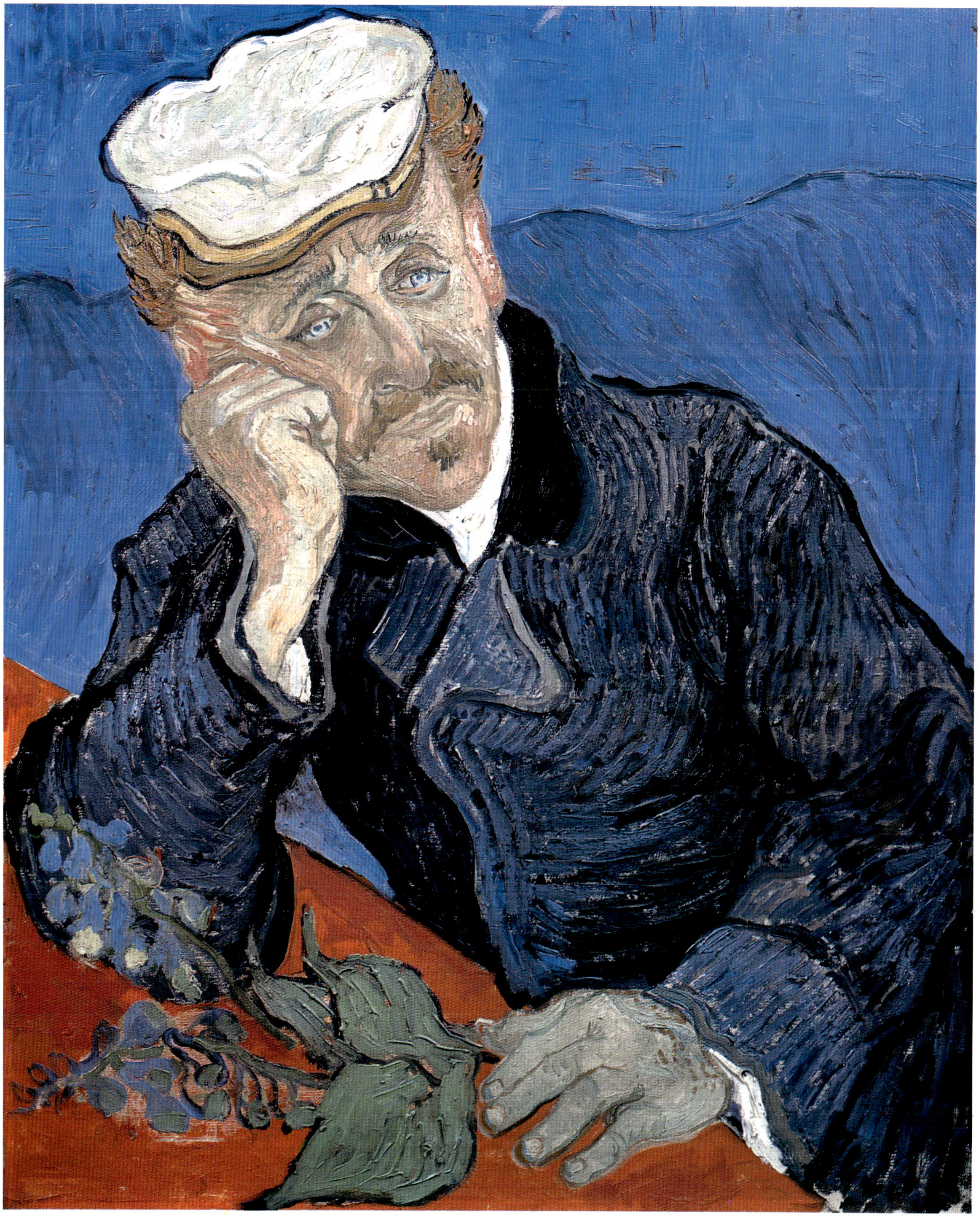

ACKNOWLEDGMENTS

The publisher would like to thank Martin Bristow, who designed this book, and Jessica Orebi Gann, who edited it. We would also like to thank the following individuals, agencies and institutions for permission to reproduce illustrations:

Foundation E G Bührle Collection, Zurich: pages 16/17
Courtauld Institute Galleries (Courtauld Collection): page 4
Dallas Museum of Art: page 13 (the Eugene and Margaret McDermott Fund in memory of Arthur Berger)
Collection of the J Paul Getty Museum, Malibu: pages 32/33
Collection of the State Museum Kröller-Müller, Otterlo: pages 14, 24/25, 28
Collection of the Museum of Modern Art, New York: pages 36/37
Reproduced by courtesy of the Trustees of the National Gallery, London: page 23
Neue Pinakothek, Munich/ARTOTHEK: page 9
Ny Carlsberg Glyptothek, Copenhagen: pages 34/35
Musée d'Orsay, Paris/photo Réunion des Musées Nationaux: pages 15, 39, 40/41, 42, 43
Vincent van Gogh Foundation/National Museum Vincent van Gogh, Amsterdam: pages 10/11, 12, 18, 19, 20/21, 22, 26/27, 29, 30/31, 38